Endorsements

With warmth and hard-won wisdom, Ann Griffiths takes readers on her lifelong leadership journey, giving us an intimate look at the seasons of wilderness, pain, wondering, growth, and joy that have shaped her—and that shape all of us as leaders. As I read her story I reflected on God's faithfulness in my own life, and I recommend this book to help you do the same.

Angie Ward
Author, *I Am a Leader: When Women Discover the Joy of Their Calling*

I enthusiastically recommend *Reignite Your Leadership Heart* to all! Ann Griffiths shares honestly the joys, disappointments, successes, and failures from her journey as a follower and servant of Jesus. Ann's wisdom, gleaned from Scripture and her own experiences, will resonate with every woman who understands her highest calling is to be a disciple of Jesus. For every man who serves Jesus, this book may help you encourage, rather than discourage, the women in your life. Ann's book is for all who desire God to use them for His Kingdom work!

Bill Taylor
Executive Director, Evangelical Free Church of Canada

Reignite Your Leadership Heart is a real, raw, and rare look behind the scenes of a church ministry trailblazer. Through seasons of doubt and discouragement, Ann Griffiths persists to overcome cultural expectations and break down barriers in the early years of the women's ministry movement. Chronicling her personal struggles and God's faithfulness to redeem her wilderness experience, Griffiths demonstrates that you don't have to be perfect to be a leader—but you do need to be resilient.

Teresa Janzen
Author, speaker, and host of Radical Abundance podcast

We all have wilderness moments when we feel lost, make mistakes, and wander from our intended path. Ann Griffiths writes like she lives—with genuine sincerity, integrity, and a passion to help others be strong leaders in their spheres of influence. With pure vulnerability, Ann shares her life's journey of success and failure. Her deeply provoking questions had me evaluating and sifting through my own thoughts and motives. I encourage everyone to make time to read Ann's story and discover faith in God's ability to *Reignite Your Leadership Heart*.

Randy Lemke
Lead Pastor, Mill Lake Church

This book reveals the heart and person of Ann Griffiths. Honesty, truth, love, and care permeate its pages. Ann's constant references to scripture and a godly focus amidst turmoil and heartache speak to her inner strength, convictions, and passion. I came away exhausted and exhilarated, weak and emotionally drained, but at peace and completely satisfied. Her words infused me with hope, strength, and trust in a perfect, sovereign, loving Almighty Heavenly Father. What more could a book do?

Bev Trainor
Educator, friend, and collaborator

Reignite Your Leadership Heart delivers on the promise of the title. Journey alongside Ann to answer her compelling call of leadership—traverse the valleys and mountain tops, sit in on the sweet fellowship with her Creator, and wander around in the parched desert far away from Him. You'll shed tears and cheer her on as she transparently shares her struggles, disappointments, encouragements, and victories; and your leadership heart will be reignited!

Athena Dean Holtz
Founder and Publisher, Redemption Press and She Writes for Him

Reignite

Your Leadership

Heart

Rise Up. Lead On.

[signature]

Joel 2:25

Reignite
Your Leadership
Heart

Inspiring Women
to Unleash
Their Full Potential

ANN GRIFFITHS

REDEMPTION
PRESS

ISBN 13: 978-1-64645-567-6 (Paperback)
        978-1-64645-566-9 (ePub)
        978-1-64645-565-2 (Mobi)
        978-1-64645-540-9 (Audiobook)

LCCN: 2022914331

Dedication

To the women who gave up for a season and
had the courage to come back.

To the women who wanted to give up
but never did.

To my husband, Jim, who didn't give up
on me—or on us.

Contents

Introduction.. xi

Part 1: Anchored in Hope

Chapter 1: Born to Make a Difference........................... 15

Chapter 2: Raised on Shoulders of Giants 23

Chapter 3: Called to Serve.. 33

Chapter 4: Preparing for Leadership.............................. 45

Part 2: Wounded But Held

Chapter 5: Collision Course... 57

Chapter 6: Cracks in the Foundation 69

Chapter 7: The Great Escape....................................... 79

Chapter 8: Running from Leadership............................. 91

Part 3: Rescued By Grace

Chapter 9: The Road Back... 103

Chapter 10: Easy Does It 113

Chapter 11: Learning to Walk Again 121

Chapter 12: Returning to Leadership 131

Part 4: Restored to Serve

Chapter 13: Invited to Lead.. 143

Chapter 14: On Trial.. 153

Chapter 15: At a Crossroad 167

One Last Word... 175

With Gratitude 177

Notes 179

Other Books by Ann Griffiths 181

Endnotes 183

Introduction

"On August 13, 1985, I felt like my life was over. But it really was only another beginning—the beginning of endless beginnings . . . a story with no end."[1]

That closing paragraph from *Grandma's Fingerprint: Love a Child. Change a Life* held the hope of new beginnings. Yet so much lurked beneath the surface. The book told the story of my journey through life with my grandma. But when people asked, "When will we see the sequel?" I could only cringe at the thought.

Would I ever be able to reveal the path my life took after Grandma's passing? Could any good come from recounting my wilderness detour that turned light into darkness? Could I get beyond the pain and embarrassment of those "wasted" years?

If they only knew.

If they only knew about the bad choices I had made. The detours I took. The heartaches I had created. If they only knew the pain I had inflicted. The trust I had betrayed. The grief I had caused. What would people think—especially those who had such hopes for me? Would they trust me in the future when they learned the truth of my past?

It has taken the passing of time and life's refining experiences for me to say, "It's time." Time to expose what I wanted to forget—

what I preferred to keep buried. Time to declare God's amazing grace that brought me out of darkness and back into the light. And time to encourage others, lost in their own wilderness and in need of that same hope and grace.

Your wilderness may be of your own making or the result of someone else's actions. Maybe you were in ministry leadership and fully committed to the call of God in your life. But somehow you found yourself wandering around in a desert place, away from God. Maybe someone betrayed your trust or you experienced hurt from other leaders or maybe even the church.

You're a wounded warrior who longs to be whole and accepted for who God created you to be. You're struggling with betrayal, doubt, fear, dishonesty, or infidelity and are no longer sure where you fit. The choices you made moved you in a direction you never imagined possible. Or maybe you don't know what plunged you into your wilderness.

I get it.

I hope that what you find here will encourage you to let go of whatever life-sapping wilderness is keeping you from unleashing the potential God placed within you. That the leader God created you to be will ignite. That the unchanging power of God's love and grace will be clear in your life.

This book is a testament to the power of God's love, mercy, and grace. It reveals a portrait of his enduring faithfulness on the mountaintop and in the wilderness wanderings of life. As you read, may you rediscover the hope that is always present, no matter where you are in your journey. May you also discover the heart and soul of what it is to be a godly leader, awaken your calling, and come to celebrate the joy of building into others.

God restored what I came to see as wasted years. Now, I invite you to let him do the same for you. He will "restore to you the years that the swarming locust has eaten" (Joel 2:25).

Part 1

ANCHORED IN HOPE

The heart and soul of a leader
begins with who we are at our core.

Born to Make a Difference

You saw me before I was born.
Every day of my life was recorded in your book.
Every moment was laid out before
a single day had passed.
Psalm 139:16 NLT

*I*t was a cloudy summer evening when my mother hurried my younger sister, baby brother, and me into a strange woman's black car. My six-year-old mind was full of questions. Why were we leaving? What would Daddy say when he got home? Who was this woman? Mommy seemed to know her, but I'd never seen her before.

We made our way along dirt roads and partially paved streets until the car made one last turn into a long, straight driveway and came to a stop. It was almost dark outside, but I knew we were at Grandma's.

There she stood. Over her clothes, Grandma wore her usual full apron with pink flowers, dark-pink edging, and a little pocket where she kept her hanky. Mommy slipped out of the car as Grandma stepped from the small, weathered wood porch and walked toward us. After a few brief words, Grandma led us into her small bungalow, and the strange woman reversed the black car out of the driveway. She was gone. We stacked our few belongings in a corner of Grandma's kitchen, and we ate a snack of toast and homemade jelly before settling into bed.

It was August 26, 1956, the day before my sister's fifth birthday, a week before I was to start school for the first time, and the day that all our lives changed. Grandma's home became our home and a hive of activity that lasted longer than one night.

In 1945, Grandma and Grandpa had purchased their property, cut trees from the land, and made boards to build their humble home. The four-room bungalow and land had still needed a lot of work when Grandpa died in 1947.

When we arrived that rainy night, almost ten years later, the outside well was the place to draw water, and the structure at the end of the pathway leading away from the house served as the toilet facilities. From the inside of Grandma's home, lonely studs revealed the exterior wall boards and cracks stuffed with newspapers or rags to keep out the cold. It was hot in summer and icy in winter. Bugs and mice continued to find their way in. To some people, her house was a shack, but to me, it was Grandma's home. And it was safe.

Since I was a two-month-old baby, my parents had left me in Grandma's care for long periods of time. I don't know all the reasons she took me in so often, but by the time we arrived on her doorstep that summer evening, I'd already spent most of my life with her. It was during those early years that a close bond formed between Grandma and me—a bond that became my anchor for years to come.

Three years, three more brothers, and many struggles later, my parents got back together "for the sake of the kids," and my dad moved in with us. One brother had been adopted out at birth, so we were five children and three adults crammed into Grandma's tiny house.

When I was eleven years old, our family moved from Grandma's, and I remember thinking, *This must be what it feels like to bleed on the inside, because it sure hurts in there right now.* That night, with my sister and brothers beside me, I lay on the floor on a well-used mattress discarded by the previous owners. It reeked of the pungent smell of dried urine and, in time, mingled its odor with secondhand cigarette smoke that washed the unpainted walls a yellowish gray.

I was a little girl who felt alone—abandoned and empty in a people-filled house with no say in where she lived. When I cried about leaving Grandma, my mother scolded me. "Don't be ridiculous. This is your home now. Forget about Grandma and go to sleep."

Brushing away the remaining tears, I whispered into the darkness, "No one will ever again see how I feel on the inside. I will never cry again."

And I didn't—until many years later. But there was a cost.

Before I turned twelve, the doctor admitted me to the hospital isolation ward and diagnosed me with having suffered a nervous breakdown. Somehow, I made it through that illness, passed into grade seven, and discovered the drums. From the moment I held a pair of drumsticks, it was as if I was born to play.

That same year, I met a teacher who traveled from school to school to teach children interested in learning to play an instrument. Though someone had only introduced me to the drums a month earlier, I signed up. Partway through grade seven, the same teacher invited me to join the senior band of high school students who came from various schools in the area. Twice a week, the teacher drove me to evening band practices, and my skills grew under his leadership. From grades seven through twelve, he affirmed my abilities. He encouraged me to learn other instruments, broaden my percussion skills, and develop my leadership. I owe a great deal to this teacher who influenced my life through music and became a lifelong friend.

Two weeks before I entered grade eight, my mom gave birth to another son. Thirteen months after that, another brother was born, and I became the eldest of eight children. Amid chaos and dysfunction, events changed the course of my life and prepared me for adventures and leadership roles beyond my imagination.

At fourteen, I attended the Canadian Sunday School Mission's Hope Bay Bible Camp on Pender Island, off the coast of British Columbia. My parents were against anything church related, so I'm not sure how I attended, but I'm sure Grandma had something to do with it. Going to Hope Bay, I felt self-conscious and struggled with low self-image. My school report cards consistently said, "Ann is conscientious and hardworking." But I was also skinny, developing physically at a slower rate than other girls, and wore clothes that seemed to hang on me. Though I didn't really know where I fit, I knew I felt great when I played the drums.

For years, Grandma battled with my parents so she could take me to Sunday school and church. She provided for me and helped me memorize Bible verses. She guided and encouraged me. Now at camp, I questioned God's role in my life and realized that relying on Grandma's faith wasn't enough. It was then that I accepted Jesus as my Savior and Lord and began my personal relationship with God. While Grandma was delighted and supported my decision, the gulf between my parents and me grew.

I'd always loved books, but it was at this stage in my life that I also began writing some of my own thoughts. One day, I wrote lyrics to a familiar tune and excitedly showed my mother.

Her only response was, "You can't write words to someone else's music."

Her disapproval cut like a knife through the fledgling writer within me. From that day on, I second-guessed everything I wrote. But I secretly continued writing. I loved words.

At fifteen, I got a job as a live-in nanny for three boys and a girl who were anything but disciplined. They were disrespectful, disobedi-ent, and hard to handle. After five months, I knew that trying to keep up with school and music and work was too difficult. Not wanting to return to my parents' house, I began the arduous task of trying to convince them to let me live with Grandma. She had significantly changed her home and welcomed the idea of having me live with her. After going back and forth with my parents and still being told they hadn't yet talked about it, I simply packed my things and walked to Grandma's. My nanny job was over, and I needed to move.

The next six weeks were wonderful until Grandma received a call from my mother, who demanded that I return to them or she would call the authorities who would take me away.

"But, Grandma, I don't want to go back."

"This time, I think you need to go," she replied. "Your mother will do what she says she will do. And I'm not sure what that could mean. It may make things difficult for you." She paused and put her arm around my shoulders. "Don't worry. I'm still here. But for now, I think it's best that you do what she says."

As we ended the evening sitting beside each other in silence, I knew Grandma was right.

It took one more year and another live-in nanny job before I finally received permission from my parents to live with Grandma. I was sixteen and remained with her until after I graduated from high school.

In my senior year, the school counselor saw a poem I had writ-ten, and asked my permission to submit it for consideration in the yearbook. When the committee chose it for publication, I thought, *Maybe I can write.* Yet the memory of my mother's words, "You can't write . . ." haunted the joy I felt. And I couldn't help but won-der, *What if I write something wrong?*

Despite a shaky foundation of upheaval, explosive uncertainty, and antagonism, there were individuals who spoke into my young life.

They encouraged me to study the Scriptures, trust God in difficult circumstances, and use my gifts and abilities. As I was always ready to try something new, I took on leadership roles at school and within the church youth group. And I grew in my faith and confidence.

The Bible is full of examples of men and women who were born to make a difference and the circumstances and people who influenced their early years. In Exodus 2:1–10, we read about the birth and young life of Moses. He came into a hostile world where the king had given the order to kill any boys born to Hebrew women. Yet, his mother kept his birth quiet for three months. Imagine keeping a baby quiet for a whole three months so the authorities would not discover him and put him to death.

Moses's mother was no fool. She was smart and trusted God. When she put her plan to save her son into motion, she likely knew that Pharaoh's daughter regularly came to a certain area to bathe. She could no longer hide Moses, so she made an unsinkable basket, laid him in it, and placed it in the river among the reeds. She also told Moses's sister to stand nearby to ensure his safety and instructed her on what to do when someone discovered him.

When Pharaoh's daughter found Moses crying, she took pity on him. As if on cue, his sister appeared, got permission to get a nurse from among the Hebrew women, and quickly brought back none other than Moses's own mother. Wow—what obedience and faith.

I can only imagine the joy that mother must have felt at being able to nurse and care for her baby without fear of him being killed. Yet I also cannot imagine her grief when the child grew and she had to deliver him to an Egyptian palace to be raised as Pharaoh's grandson.

We hear nothing more about Moses's mother, but it seems she was an honorable woman. She trusted God, followed through on her commitment to Pharaoh's daughter, and sacrificed her joy for her son's future. She had no way of knowing the significant role her son would play in God's greater plan for his people. But she was faithful.

Moses went on to be educated and raised for leadership in Egypt, but not before he was first influenced by his Hebrew parents and others who would have been around him.

Each of us is born to make a difference and are affected by our upbringing. Some experiences and individuals influence us positively, while others appear to have a negative impact. Either way, God is faithful through all generations. He has a good and greater plan.

As I think back on the men and women who spoke into my young life—people who encouraged, mentored, corrected, and inspired me—I'm in awe. I'm grateful. The road was sometimes rough and unpredictable, but all along, God was there.

Just prior to my high school graduation, I took a further step in my walk with God by being baptized in a public service with Grandma standing by. That commitment would be deeply tested in years to come.

Raised on Shoulders of Giants

*If I have seen further, it is by
standing on the shoulders of giants.*
—Isaac Newton

Leadership takes many forms. It can raise us up or tear us down. But in all cases, it's spelled i-n-f-l-u-e-n-c-e. Influence. During the summer before my high school graduation, I traveled with two friends to a village in northern Saskatchewan. The trip took two days by bus to go two provinces east of where we lived. At barely seventeen years of age, I was thrust into unknown territory. When we arrived to help missionaries with summer meetings and camps, we discovered we had to develop our own lessons and prepare materials out of whatever was available. I was grateful for the times I had previously spent helping my grandma when she taught vacation Bible school at our church.

After almost a month, my friends returned home, but I continued touring the province with a small team, teaching at vacation Bible schools and working as a counselor or support crew at Bible camps. The entire summer made such an impression on me that the year following high school graduation, I returned by myself to do it all over again.

Those two summers were a powerful training ground that fueled my desire to trust God more. When asked to teach and lead teens not much younger than me, I had no choice but to trust him. Thankfully, God also provided mentors who guided my leadership and teaching.

After graduating from high school, I didn't know exactly what to do. I dismissed the idea of attending university to study music, although it would continue to be a part of my life. I also contemplated Bible school but wasn't sure about where to go. At the end of that second summer of working in camps and vacation Bible schools, I returned home with a longing to go back to the small northern town of Big River, Saskatchewan, where I'd become friends with a large Christian family. I didn't know how I'd support myself but knew that God had something for me to do there. I just needed to step into the challenge.

I had no money and no job lined up, but I had a bus ticket in hand and room and board arranged at the Carter home for $30 a month. It was a small amount even for the times, but a lot for me. I also had Grandma's blessing once she was sure I was going to a safe home. So, off I went again on another adventure, not knowing what lay ahead or how much stretching my faith would experience.

The job I secured came after I spent a couple of days walking up and down the main street, asking God which of the limited businesses I should approach. When I settled on one of two cafés in town, I stood across the street and watched who went in and out. I'd been told the owners likely wouldn't hire because they had their own family of twelve children to help.

When I finally worked up the courage to walk into the bustling hot spot of town, they hired me on the spot—for ninety-five cents an hour. My first job was washing dishes by hand, but I was soon also cleaning floors, serving tables, and stocking food deliveries. Grandma had taught me that every job needed to be done with excellence—even though it wasn't very glamorous. God had provided a job with enough income to meet my commitments and placed me right in the middle of town. Workers and businesspeople gathered at the café in the daytime, and teenagers congregated late in the day and evening. It was the perfect place to make connections and invite teens to the youth activities at the small church I attended with the Carters, who made up most of the congregation.

The Carter home became my bootcamp. There I learned to live with a small-town, conservative Christian family who held opinions and taboos in stark contrast to those I grew up with. Yet, I also watched and listened as a deep love and respect for each other overshadowed the rules. I witnessed Christlike behavior that affected a whole town. And I enjoyed being a part of discussions with visiting missionaries, pastors, and Bible school students who were constant guests around the family table. The Carters may not have been materially wealthy, but they firmly believed God would provide all they needed. There was always room for one more person at the table and enough of anything to share—even if all they could do was add a little water to the soup.

Unfortunately, something else I came to realize while living under the roof of the Carter family was that I had a bit of a rebellious spirit. Thankfully, God was gracious, and the Carters were patient.

After a full year in Big River with the Carters, I traveled home to British Columbia to spend a couple of weeks with Grandma and friends before returning to Saskatchewan. This time it was to the southern part of the province and a different way of living—Bible school dorm life. I attended for only one year, but in that year, I received solid biblical teaching from dedicated teachers, helped pioneer a coffeehouse ministry to reach community teens with the gospel, and heard visiting speakers who were making a difference in various parts of the world.

Our dean of women was a tall, gray-haired missionary who had become widowed while on the mission field. She'd returned home with her two children and soon gained a strict, no-nonsense reputation among the school's students and faculty. It didn't take long to realize she saw right through my subtle flashes of rebellion whenever I pushed the rule book boundaries or instigated dorm pranks. Her example taught me that a calm response can often be more effective than a long lecture and stern look, although they too may have their place. She also taught me that what's in the heart of a person affects how she acts—even when she's being foolish.

Her subtle smile at our dorm pranks showed me that fun was fun, but a person must be accountable and take responsibility for the outcome of the fun. She made a lasting impression on me and became another pair of shoulders in a long string of giants God used to mold me into the person he knew was there but whom I had not yet seen.

At the end of the school year, I returned home to spend the summer with Grandma and work as the volunteer assistant to Len Roberts, the first youth pastor of my home church. That experience launched a lifelong friendship with Len and his wife, Jean, and years of doing ministry together. While we rolled up our sleeves to renovate the old section of the church and turn it into a coffee-house and youth center, we also brainstormed ideas. It was Len who taught me to plan strategically. To think outside the box and organize teams to focus them on a vision. To look at ministry and everyday life as one, rather than two separate parts of life.

When the Missing Link Coffeehouse opened in the fall, I knew I would not return to Bible school. Instead, I got a paying job and continued volunteering at the church where we saw upward of three hundred teens come through the coffeehouse doors each weekend. I continued assisting Len and became the drummer in the house band, which also began playing at other churches and outdoor youth events. It was a learning and serving time—a time of being on the cutting edge and making a difference. And I loved it.

During this same time, a friendship with a handsome sailor developed. We'd first met when I was sixteen but had gone our separate ways before meeting up again a year later. Jim had a way about him that contradicted people's perceptions of someone who wore a leather jacket and rode a motorcycle. He had black hair and eyes that were dark, deep set, and kind. He stood tall and straight with a gentle yet edgy appeal that fascinated me. Fresh out of the navy, apprenticing as a bricklayer, and desiring to live for God, he volunteered with us at the coffeehouse. In 1971, we were married, and a new adventure began. He was twenty-four, and I was twenty-one.

A month after we were married, Jim told me he'd been up most of the night and believed God wanted him to go to university. Over the next two years, we witnessed miracle after miracle of God's provision. I worked on campus; he attended classes and took odd jobs, and we continued volunteering at the coffeehouse.

As Jim was about to start his third year, Len Roberts approached us with a proposal that would forever change our life direction. "I've resigned from the church and would like you to consider taking a year off university to help start a ministry to reach underprivileged youth and young offenders. What do you think?"

After talking and praying about it, we took the plunge. The new ministry became One Way Adventure Foundation and was another bootcamp where God continued to hone my skills, refine my walk with him, and stretch my faith. But it would not be without challenges.

In 1973, we moved from our small university campus apartment to a three-level rental townhouse where our home became a constant stream of people. I never knew who would be around for dinner but was grateful to the Carters for showing me how to stretch a meal. We took in a boarder to help make ends meet. As another part of our ministry, Len and Jean and Jim and I became government-approved foster parents.

It was official. We were foster parents to teenagers before having any children of our own. The boys we fostered were known to the police and ranged in age from fourteen to sixteen. Their families had given up on them, and they'd experienced every program available to them, including juvenile detention. They were con artists, drug addicts, and break-and-enter felons. On one occasion, we had a boy living with us who was involved with the occult and another boy suspected of attempting to kill his parents. But they each needed a safe home environment with discipline and boundaries wrapped in unconditional love.

Within less than a year, the ministry supported twelve to fifteen staff and had about forty teens involved in day programs. As the demand grew, Len heard of property in a small town about two hundred miles away and, by faith, purchased it. We were on the move again.

I was pregnant with our first child when Jim and I moved to the small hamlet of Hedley, British Columbia, to oversee the work while Len and Jean remained behind to continue operating the base ministry. Initially, we lived in one room and cooked our meals on a camp stove, along with a second couple who lived in another room with their toddler. Within a couple of months, Jim and I moved into a twelve-by-sixty-eight-foot mobile home, which we shared with another couple and their son. We also continued to foster and provide meals for junior staff.

Over the next three and a half years, the ministry grew considerably, and God blessed us with a daughter and son. Sarah was born with a medical condition that required special care during the first couple years of her life but thankfully left no lasting effects. Seventeen months later, James was born. When he never seemed to stop crying, the doctor informed me he had severe colic. This condition lasted four and a half months, and life became even more complicated.

The pace was relentless. Responsibilities for babies, teenagers, meals, and a stream of people were all never ending. I could feel myself sinking, and though I didn't fully understand it, I now believe I was on the edge of my first serious wilderness experience. It was then that God taught me a valuable lesson.

One particularly difficult day, I sat on the floor looking at the rows of books along the wall of our mobile home living room. I remember hearing myself say, "God, I need something—anything to get me through this."

I loved books, but it seemed like an eternity since I'd had time or energy to read. Scanning the shelves, my eyes landed on a hardcover book titled *Something More* by Catherine Marshall. That book became another pair of shoulders for me to stand on.

Over the next few days, I devoured the book, and God showed me a different perspective on my life. He reminded me I was his child, and he knew all about what was going on. He brought me this far and was still holding me in his love. Nothing could touch me unless he stepped aside and allowed it. His purpose was for my growth and his glory. I simply needed to acknowledge his presence and thank and praise him for what was happening in my life.

"Okay, Lord, I acknowledge your presence and thank you for all that's happening right now. But, Lord, you want me to praise you for it? How do I do that?"

Later that day, I was washing dishes at the kitchen sink and glanced out the window at the desert-like soil and rocks that surrounded our mobile home. Tuffs of grass poked up between the rocks, and I could only imagine the beautiful red and yellow and orange flowers I would plant—if only I had the time.

With my hands in dishwater, I noticed a single wildflower standing alone among the rocks and sand. It was waving gently in the breeze as if to say, "Here I am, Ann. God made me too." I thought about what I'd been reading and realized that God was telling me I could start praising him for the little things—even a single wildflower in the dust.

Eventually, I moved from thanking and praising him for one lone flower to thanking and praising him for all he allowed in my life and what he would do with it—in his time.

Almost ten years had passed since my high school graduation. They were years of change, adventure, and growth. Years when God stretched and molded me and chipped and ground away at some of my rough edges. Notice I said *some*. And they were years when the words and actions of faith giants lifted me up and challenged me to spread my wings.

Many heroes of the faith—both biblical characters and everyday, ordinary people were raised up on the shoulders of giants. But we often forget that those giants also had giants in their lives—people who mentored, advised, corrected, and guided them. Generations of giants influencing more giants like you and me.

In First and Second Kings, we read the story of two giants named Elijah and Elisha. Elijah was an in-your-face kind of prophet, chosen by God to confront evil head-on. He was obedient, courageous, and passionate about his mission to turn people away from idolatry and back to God.

Conversely, Elisha spent less of his time confronting evil and more time showing compassion to people. He demonstrated the powerful side of God and performed more miracles than Elijah, but he also revealed God's caring and compassionate nature.

When God directed Elijah to anoint Elisha to succeed him, Elijah didn't complain or question God's wisdom about who was to be his successor. Effectively, God said, "This is your replacement, Elijah. Walk with him and mentor him. When he's ready to take your place, I'll let you know."

Elijah had learned to trust God. All he had to do was take the first step, and the rest would follow. When was the last time God asked you to take just one step without you knowing where it would lead?

Elijah also didn't approach Elisha with the attitude of "Watch and learn, kid." Rather, he simply obeyed, and Elisha "went after Elijah and assisted him" (1 Kings 19:21).

As the two traveled together and witnessed the power of God and his miracles, their mentor-mentee relationship became a friendship bond that lasted until God declared, "It's time."

Can you imagine their conversations as they set out from Gilgal on what was to be their last walk together? Would they have recounted God's hand on their lives? Would they have reflected on God's faithfulness during periods of mutual silence? Or would they have simply been in awe of God's greatness?

This last journey tells us a lot about Elisha. First, he was loyal. As they walked from Gilgal to Bethel and then to Jericho and across the Jordan River, it's as if Elijah wanted to protect Elisha from the inevitable.

Three times, he told him, "Elisha, please stay here."

But Elisha would have none of it. Each time he replied, "I will not leave you."

I wonder if he thought, *We've grown close over the years and cared for each other. Why abandon you on this last leg of the journey?*

In three different places along their journey, prophets told him, "Don't you know the Lord is going to take your master from you today?"

But Elisha didn't flinch. "Of course I know. Now be quiet about it."

Was he avoiding the inevitable? Or did he simply not want anything to disturb their last moments together?

When they finally crossed the Jordan River, Elijah asked Elisha,

"Tell me what I can do for you before I am taken away."

That's where we see that Elisha was a big thinker and not afraid to speak up. Without hesitation, Elisha replied, "Please let there be a double portion of your spirit on me" (2 Kings 2:9).

This is significant. According to custom, it was the firstborn son who received a double portion of the father's inheritance. Elisha was asking to be Elijah's heir or successor. But that decision was God's. Elisha could only watch and wait.

When Elisha finally witnessed Elijah being taken up to heaven in a whirlwind, we see in 2 Kings 2:12–13 that he cried and tore his clothes. Elisha grieved deeply at the loss of his mentor and friend. Yet, he did not take his eyes off God.

The very next verse tells us Elisha picked up Elijah's cloak and struck the Jordan River with it, just as he had seen Elijah do earlier.

When the water divided and he crossed the river, the prophets from Jericho watched and declared, "The spirit of Elijah rests on Elisha" (2 Kings 2:15).

God granted Elisha's request because his motives were pure. He wasn't interested in being better or more powerful than Elijah. Elisha simply wanted God to fulfill his purposes through him just as he saw them fulfilled through Elijah. Elisha stood on the shoulders of a giant and would soon raise others on his shoulders. But he knelt on his face before God.

Think about the giants God used to mold you into the influential leader he created you to be. What would they say to you now?

During the first quarter century of my life, God used individuals and books to teach me valuable leadership lessons. And, yes, he even used a little flower outside my window. But he wasn't yet finished.

Called to Serve

There are no limits set to the power of God
given to the least of us.
—Amy Carmichael

Throughout my life, I loved reading stories about people who made a difference in the world. I enjoyed conversations with individuals who challenged my thinking too. But in those early years of motherhood, the idea of leadership didn't enter my mind. I didn't consider myself a leader in the sense that many of us think of a leader. True, I had been in leadership positions throughout my teens and early twenties, but things changed when I entered the season of children, home, and supporting my husband in his ministry role.

Daily diapers and laundry. Cooking upward of six meals a day to meet the varied schedules of those who ate at our table. Cleaning up household messes. Settling sibling squabbles and myriad demands beyond parenthood. It was enough to keep any man or woman scrambling.

Following the births of our two children, we twisted our way through a maze of doctors and hospitals, ministry and work, moving and school. We had initially committed to take one year away from Jim's studies to help start the ministry of One Way Adventure Foundation. But when one year turned into four years and two babies, God nudged us to get Jim back to his third year of university.

Every Sunday throughout the fall, we traveled two hundred miles from the One Way facilities in Hedley, BC, to stay with my grandma while Jim studied and attended classes at nearby Simon Fraser University during the week. Each Friday, our little family then drove back to the One Way campus to host camps and retreats over the weekend.

By Christmas 1977, we lived at Grandma's most of the time. Jim continued his studies, and because I started an on-call job at the public library, he traveled to Hedley by himself on weekends. Grandma, Jim, and I constantly juggled our schedules so one of us could be with the children. Flexibility and grace were a must.

Once that university year was complete, we moved back to Hedley to work for the summer. Our responsibilities included the operations of camps and retreat groups and hosting a bed-and-breakfast in the main building known as Colonial Lodge.

Our little family of four took up residence in the lodge in a twelve-by-twelve room with an attached bathroom. The room opened onto the lobby of the lodge and put us right in the epicenter of activity that included groups coming and going for camps and retreats, bed-and-breakfast guests, the central office, and multiple staff and resident teens. When there were guests, we provided breakfast, cleaned rooms, and mingled with visitors in the evening over a cup of tea. Every Sunday night, One Way staff and teens-in-care gathered in the lodge for church.

Our two children, now two and three years old, quickly learned to interact with people of all ages and from different walks of life. They also learned that while they had the run of the lodge when guests weren't around, strict rules and boundaries applied when visitors arrived. Again, flexibility was key.

At the end of the summer, we decided it was better for the children if I stayed with them at the lodge to continue our work while Jim returned to university. Each Sunday, he boarded a bus in Hedley for a trip to my grandma's that took about five hours. The following Friday, he then did the trip all over again to return to us for the weekend. Though I was pretty self-sufficient and independent, sometimes I was uneasy, especially when there were no guests and the children and I were the only ones in the rambling three-story, early twentieth century Colonial Lodge.

One night, the three of us were asleep in our tiny room when I heard glass breaking in the building. My eyelids flew open and my heart raced. As I lay in my pull-out couch bed, I strained to hear something—anything. But nothing broke the still of the night.

"I guess it was nothing," I whispered to myself. Looking over at the thick oak door that separated our room from the rest of the lodge, I closed my eyes. *Crash.* There it was again.

Quietly, I got out of bed, checked that the children were still asleep, and made my way to the door. Should I open it? What would I see? It was pitch black. Had a lamp tipped over? Had a large bowl fallen off a shelf in the kitchen? Maybe a window had shattered?

When I heard nothing more, I gingerly opened the door and, with a flashlight in hand, walked toward the living room and the sound of the crash. Everything was quiet and in order. There was nothing broken and no one in sight. Yet, something in my spirit said I wasn't alone. Wary to venture farther, I walked back into our room, locked the door, and lay awake until sunrise.

In the morning, I walked from room to room and found nothing out of place. As staff arrived, I questioned them and relayed my experience. No one had been near the building. When Jim arrived for the weekend, I also told him what had happened. Each time I recounted the experience and rehearsed it in my mind, I asked myself, *Did I imagine it? Was it a dream?* In the end, I concluded it was real. I just couldn't explain it naturally.

After four months of Jim's going back and forth, we realized it was much harder for our family to be separated than we'd expected.

On January 2, 1979, we relocated to the coast, where Grandma welcomed us with open arms. Within five days, we moved into a two-bedroom apartment in the men's dorm of Trinity Western University, and I started a part-time job in the library. In lieu of rent, we served as dorm supervisors, which meant unlocking and locking the outer doors every morning and evening, vacuuming the halls and stairways, and keeping the common laundry room clean. Jim continued in his final year at Simon Fraser University and worked with One Way at their local office.

During the first eight years of our marriage, God performed miracle after miracle as we obeyed him in ministry. But as my February 7, 1979, journal entry attests, it wasn't always easy.

What have I gotten myself into? If Jim had been in school before we got married, would it have made a difference? I thought I was marrying a bricklayer, not a budding psychologist . . . It didn't matter how tiny our one-bedroom apartment was. We didn't mind concocting different ways to eat macaroni or hamburger. We were a young couple with no other demanding responsibilities but each other, Jim's studies, and my job. A couple with a lot of dreams . . . Now it's two part-time jobs, supervising a single men's college residence, a full load of studies, more bills to pay, and two small children to guide along the way.

Life had become a blur. Little did I know God was using those experiences to prepare me for even greater leaps of faith.

After eight months of living in the men's dorm, I struggled with feelings that I had accomplished nothing with my life. True, I married a wonderful guy, abandoned my education to help him through university, worked in many facets of full-time ministry, fostered several teenage boys, and had two children. But what had I really done with my life?

Even as a young girl, I dreamed of leaving a mark on the world, besides a gravestone. But now, I wondered if that mark would reveal itself in my two children, and what they would eventually do with their lives. At twenty-nine, I thought time was running out. I loved my marriage and my children, but I also felt like there was something more for me to do.

Whether Grandma sensed my restlessness or God whispered in her ear, I don't know. Maybe both. Either way, she stepped up, invited me to a women's event, and encouraged me to get involved with the women at the church where I grew up and she served as an active charter member. Almost immediately, I began attending meetings, pitching in where needed, and developing friendships with godly women.

During that same year, I started a business selling books through a Christian book company to augment our income. The business became financially successful with a bright future ahead. But by the end of 1980, I sensed God leading me away from business and calling me to work with women.

When I told a business associate why I was letting the business go, she said, "Are you crazy? You want to work with women? They've got to be the hardest group in the world to work with."

I had no idea what ministry to women meant or what it entailed. I only knew God captured my attention and catapulted my focus toward what it seemed he'd prepared me for all along.

Meanwhile, Jim finished his BA honors degree in the summer of 1979 and we moved off the Trinity Western campus. Our first-born started kindergarten while Jim continued working with One Way Adventure Foundation and leading a new division to assist young men who had suffered serious brain injuries. They, too, became regular faces in our home as Jim helped them relearn social skills and explore new job possibilities.

In early 1981, Grandma sold her home, and we purchased a duplex together. It was a wonderful arrangement with Grandma living on one side and our little family on the other. During this time, Youth for Christ Vancouver approached Jim to head up their youth guidance division, working with families and kids on the streets and from low-income areas.

It was a tough decision. For seven years, God had taken us on an incredible journey with One Way. We grew in ways we never imagined possible and felt deep loyalty to our friends, Len and Jean, and the other staff who now numbered about sixty men and women. How could we leave?

My writing during that period of decision-making gives evidence of the turmoil we were feeling. In an open letter to the women of our church, I wrote what I thought was for them, but I now believe I was speaking more to myself:

Sifting keeps us constantly looking to God for direction. (Should we go this way or that?) Sometimes, a little encouragement to "enlarge our borders" is necessary.

As we prayed and talked, we reasoned that going with Youth for Christ would primarily require Jim's time. I'd be able to pursue other interests and care for our children, who were now becoming involved with school and community activities. Together, we'd raise our financial support, communicate with donors, and attend functions.

Five months after moving into our duplex with Grandma, and after a lot of prayer and discussions with key people in our lives, we committed to Youth for Christ. Jim began work with them in June 1981—the same month and year that I began a new-to-me leadership role.

Within a year and a half of Grandma inviting me to a women's event, and shortly after ending my profitable business venture, the church women asked me to lead the executive team. It was then that God filled me with passion, vision, and new ideas to help women grow in Christ and reach beyond the church walls. It was time for change during changing times.

At thirty-one years of age, I became president of the church women's group with two immediate challenges to address. First, to bring the women's executives together as a solid team under a young leader. Second, to determine how best to move from a traditional women's missionary society format to something broader known as women's ministries. The transition had the potential to divide or energize. But rather than tear down the foundation laid by faithful pioneering women like my grandma, we built on their foundation and included them in the planning and implementation.

At the close of our first year, I wrote:

We need a broader vision of our ministry to women in the church and community—a continual awareness of the needs of the women and a constant seeking of ways to meet those needs . . . it means a giving of ourselves to others and for others.

And we gave.

Women got involved. Activities mushroomed. And individuals grew in Christ. I learned how to communicate a vision and rally individuals to implement that vision. And I began to understand the importance of moving fast enough to make progress, yet slow enough to keep everyone together.

At the end of that first year, I received a request to serve as district president for our denomination's women's groups. Some groups were operating under decades-old conventional methods while others had adopted some changes. Bringing them together—and all heading in the same direction while honoring where each group was in their ministry—was the challenge we faced. When I was sworn in to my new role, Grandma said a few words. In her notes, which I've kept to this day, her last line read, "I think Ann was born to be a leader."

Have you ever had someone say that about you? Have you ever had someone encourage you to step into a leadership role outside your family? It's a humbling experience and a charge not to be taken lightly.

Traveling to speak at various groups while working with a wonderful team of women, I carried out my duties in the district for the next two years. During those two years, from 1982 to 1984, I also continued leading our church women's group with another amazing team of women.

Obligations forced me closer to God as I realized my own inadequacies and need for his wisdom and guidance. My desire was for God to continue his work in and through me—wherever he chose, whenever he chose, and in whatever way he chose. However, that desire was soon to be tested, as God once more stretched my faith and reminded me that whom he calls he equips for the task.

In 1983, the executive director of our denomination's national office asked my mentor and friend, Eileen Enarson, to form a task force to establish a national women's organization for the denomination. She had been a pastor's wife, speaker, broadcaster, and national president of our women's US counterpart. She oozed years of leadership experience. When the task force neared the end of their one-year commitment, they invited me to sit in on the writing of the constitution and bylaws. Working with such a team of wise and experienced women was an incredible and humbling honor.

Within a few short weeks, Eileen and the task force sat me down and said, "We believe God wants you to be the first president of this new national organization."

"Me? But I'm only thirty-three years old. There are other women, far more qualified women, with more knowledge and experience than me. Any of you, for example."

"No. We believe God has chosen you. Think about it, and we'll pray with you as you decide."

You bet I prayed. And I talked with my family. It was an enormous commitment and responsibility that would require travel and time. As I considered my decision, excitement grew within me, and I realized God had already been paving the way.

Before the task force approached me, I had given notice that, after serving as chair of our church women's group for three years, I believed it was time to step down. My two-year term as president of the district women's organization was also ending. It appeared God was clearing my schedule and preparing my heart for a new assignment. I said yes.

The 1984 national conference marked significant milestones. It was the one hundredth anniversary of our denomination in North America. The year in which ninety-five Canadian churches assumed full responsibility for their own autonomous ministry. The year they commissioned me as president of Women's Ministries of Canada, along with six other women who stood with me to serve as the first national board.[2]

Reflecting on those years, I know God blessed me with an incredibly dedicated, gifted, and fun team. Together, we accomplished more in three years than anyone expected. To this day, I treasure them as special friends.

From 1981 to 1984, it was one adventure after another. Sometimes it felt like God had dropped me in the middle of a storm at sea and said, "Go to work." Other times, he cradled me in his arms and whispered, "Rest a while." Whether in the storm or the shelter, his mighty arms held me—lifting, carrying, and guiding me along.

I wonder if that's how Joshua felt when God told Moses to, "Take Joshua, son of Nun, who has the Spirit in him, and lay your hands on him. Present him to Eleazar the priest before the whole community, and publicly commission him to lead the people" (Numbers 27:18–19 NLT).

As Moses neared the end of his 120 years on earth, he prayed and asked God to help him find a replacement. He didn't want the people to be left without a leader. When God told him it was to be Joshua, Moses didn't whisper it in secret. And he didn't wait until his death to make it known to the people.

When God said, "It's Joshua who will succeed you," Moses did exactly what God told him to do—lay his hands on him, present him to the priest, and commission him in the sight of everyone.

The first mention of Joshua is in Exodus 17:9, where we see him leading men into battle under the direction of Moses. Little did anyone know then that God had him in training to become Moses's replacement. That he would lead the Israelites into even greater battles when they crossed the Jordan into the land God promised them.

According to Joshua 1:1, Joshua was also Moses's assistant. With the teaching and experience he gained under Moses's mentorship and the Spirit of God within him, Joshua grew in faith.

Joshua didn't have to sit in the wings before he rolled up his sleeves and got to work as Israel's leader-in-waiting. God instructed Moses to transfer some of his authority to Joshua so the whole community of Israel would obey him (Numbers 27:20 NLT). Again, Moses was obedient and assigned responsibilities to Joshua, which made transitioning leadership easier for all involved.

Moses trusted God and showed confidence in Joshua, who had certainly proven himself in the past. For example, Numbers 13:1–14:30 tells the story of twelve men sneaking into the promised land to see what Israel would soon be up against. Only Caleb and Joshua believed God would help Israel conquer the land.

God did not leave Joshua on his own to sink or swim in his new role. He told Moses, "When direction from the Lord is needed, Joshua will stand before Eleazar the priest, who will use the Urim—one of the sacred lots cast before the Lord—to determine his will. This is how Joshua and the rest of the community of Israel will determine everything they should do" (Numbers 27:21 NLT). As Israel's future leader, Joshua was not abandoned by God. Joshua had the support of Moses, Eleazar, and the entire community of Israel because he was God's chosen man for the job.

But though Joshua's faith was strong, Deuteronomy 31:7–8 tells us that Moses instructed him not once, but twice, to be strong and courageous. After Moses's death, we see in Joshua 1:6–9, that God told Joshua not only to be strong and courageous but to, "be strong and very courageous." Joshua had faith God would fulfill all he promised, but finding courage to deal with everything he'd have to face in the future was going to be a challenge.

Maybe you're in a season of life that makes taking on a leadership role seem farfetched. Or maybe you know God gifted and called you to lead, but you don't know where you fit. Maybe you're fully engaged in leadership and loving every minute. Well, almost every minute. Maybe you're a leader who's struggling in a wilderness or desert place and you're not sure you can keep going. Or maybe you think life would be so much easier if you simply sat in the back row and let others get on with it.

In the early years of my leadership journey, God used challenges and individuals to mold and build my faith. Eileen Enarson, who headed up the task force to form Women's Ministries of Canada, stands out as my Moses. She encouraged and taught me through her words and by her example. God used her to achieve so much in her lifetime, and she could easily have taken on the new role of president. Instead, she took a young woman under her wing and mentored her in godly leadership. I will always be thankful for her trust and friendship.

When I think back to the national conference that commissioned our little group of seven to serve together as a national board, I still see the smile on Eileen's face and hear the sincerity in her prayer of commitment as she dedicated us to the work ahead. Once we began, she provided wise counsel and support when asked, and did not hover or try to control our progress.

Eileen is now nearing her one hundredth birthday. Yet, after all those years when we finish talking together, she still does not say goodbye. Instead, she says, "To be continued."

Each leadership journey takes twists and turns, as mine was soon to take. But I came to realize that each bend in the road is a "to be continued."

Chapter 4

Preparing for Leadership

If you have influence, you are a leader.
—Angie Ward

Since the dawn of time, God has placed individuals in strategic places and given them abilities to fulfill what he called them to accomplish. Among those people are women who, against all odds, filled unique and vital leadership roles.

From biblical times, Scripture recounts stories of women from various walks of life who stepped forward to lead. Women like Deborah who led an army to victory. Queen Esther, who put her life on the line and ultimately saved her people. Ruth, whom Israelites considered a foreigner, but who ultimately became the great-grandmother of King David and found her place in the lineage of Jesus. Leaders like Anna, who spoke for God in the temple and ranked among the first to acknowledge Jesus as the Messiah. Lydia, who was an influential businesswoman. Dorcas, who used a needle and thread to make a living and serve the poor. Priscilla, who mentored and taught other leaders. And so many more.

In our recent history, there are countless women who obeyed God's call and stepped into leadership. Some stepped boldly. Some hesitantly. And some fearfully. Women like Amy Carmichael, Corrie ten Boom, Elisabeth Elliot, Joni Eareckson Tada, Mother Teresa, Rosa Parks, and Ruth Bell Graham. Or women like Elinor Young, Helen Roseveare, Henrietta Mears, and Faye Edgerton. Some have become household names while others are less familiar.

Some women faced disappointment with courage and grit. Women like Mary McLeod Bethune, whose goal was to be a missionary in Africa. When she was told there were no openings for "Negro missionaries" in Africa, she recalled saying, "Africans in America needed Christ and school just as much as Negroes in Africa . . . My life work lay not in Africa, but in my own country." Mary's accomplishments ranged from starting schools and hospitals to becoming president of Bethune-Cookman College, founder of the National Council of Negro Women, special adviser to three United States presidents, and more.[3]

Some women were determined to go their own way until God showed them otherwise. Dr. Ida Scudder vowed never to follow in her missionary family's footsteps. When she stopped wrestling with God, she attended medical school and returned to India where she had been born. There, she treated female patients and trained Indian women to become doctors and nurses. From a single bed dispensary, she developed what is now one of India's largest and most prominent medical facilities.[4]

There are many generations of women whose stories are worthy of being told, but that would require many more books. Some women made a difference in their local areas, while others had a worldwide impact. Many had humble beginnings and overcame extreme hardships. Most, if not all, of their stories led them in ways they could never have imagined.

Today is no different. We each have a story—grief, joy, sickness, defeat, confusion, adventure, betrayal, and victory. It's all there. We may be in business, ministry, politics, the arts, or advocacy. We may serve at home or in another country. Whom God calls, he directs and sustains. All he asks is that we obediently stand in the place he created us to fill in history. Each of us will probably take a different path to get there, but in all cases, he knows the way we must take to bring glory to him.

As I continue the story of God's patience and faithfulness in my life to date, I trust God will lift you up by his mercy, empower you by his grace, and embolden you by the hope that he alone brings.

Before we close this first section, Anchored in Hope, let's look at five principles that are important to anyone starting out on their amazing leadership journey.

Be Curious

Growing up, I asked lots of questions. When I couldn't get answers from the adults in my life, I found a book that gave them to me. Usually, that meant taking a walk to the bookmobile that traveled to outlying communities with no public library. Every couple of weeks, it stopped near the corner of our street and the main road. There, I waited in line for my turn to enter the small bus that had been transformed into a library. Oh, how I loved that mobile library.

When it was my turn, the driver, who was also the librarian, motioned me in. I'd make my way up the couple of steps and enter a paradise of books lining every inside wall, leaving little room for two patrons. I enjoyed times when there weren't many people in line and I could leisurely search the shelves for interesting subjects to explore. If what I was looking for wasn't there, I'd put in a request and the librarian would bring options on the next run.

But being curious is not just about asking questions and devouring books. It's about being open to change and looking beyond the obvious. Some people find this task difficult. They're not able to settle on a house to buy or rent because they don't like the color of the kitchen walls. Or they don't want to pull up stakes and move to another city or neighborhood. They're root people. They put their roots down and determine to keep them there.

These scenarios may represent personal preferences or idiosyncrasies, but when they hinder us from stepping out in obedience to God's leading in our lives, that's serious business.

How many times have you missed out on an opportunity or adventure God called you to fulfill? You put your head down and said, "No thanks. Not today. I'm not the least bit curious. I'm comfortable right here, happy doing what I'm doing."

The Queen of Sheba was curious. In 1 Kings 10:1–13, we read about how her curiosity led her to seek after a man who trusted the God of Israel. Was King Solomon everything she'd been told? Were the stories true? Her curiosity and willingness to be uprooted from her homeland exposed her to the true source of Solomon's wisdom. After testing him with hard questions, she went away, convinced she'd only heard half of his greatness.

When we seek God's wisdom, he guides the questions, reveals the answers, and enlightens our thoughts.

"Getting wisdom is the wisest thing you can do" (Proverbs 4:7 NLT).

Be Teachable

When did you last ask a question and not like the answer? You wanted someone's advice, but when they gave it, you didn't want to hear it. That's curiosity without teachability.

It's like saying, "I want your advice, but I don't plan to take it. I want to know what you have to tell me, but I don't want to listen." How often do we do that with each other? How often do we do that with God?

Listening is an art. Being a good listener is a skill. We hear words without really listening to what's being said. We hear words without watching what the body is telling us. And we hear words without listening between the lines to know what someone is really trying to tell us. When we hear only with our ears and not our heart, we aren't really listening. We're not being teachable.

Being teachable is also a skill and an art. While we can be a student of good books and a brilliant conversationalist, if we don't have a teachable heart to absorb and apply what we're being taught, we're simply taking in information. We exercise our mind while our heart becomes dull.

You know the story about Martha in Luke 10:38–42 inviting Jesus and his disciples to her home. She went about busying herself with all the meal preparations. Meanwhile, her sister Mary sat quietly, listening to Jesus. When Martha complained about Mary not helping her, Jesus said, "My dear Martha, you are worried and upset over all these details. There is only one thing worth being concerned about. Mary has discovered it, and it will not be taken away from her."

Have you ever wondered what Martha did after Jesus rebuked her? Martha's attitude shows up again in the story of Lazarus, found in John 11:17–44. Here, Martha makes sure Jesus knows he's late, and that Lazarus has been dead for four days. She wanted to make sure Jesus knew the details of the situation. But Jesus replied, "Didn't I tell you that you would see God's glory if you believe?"

Being detail oriented and a bit of a perfectionist myself, I've often thought that, down through time, we've painted Martha with a bad brush. She wasn't bad. She just had her priorities mixed up and her attention to detail kept her from seeing the big picture. But I believe Martha was teachable. John 11:27 suggests she was a woman of deep faith, when she answered Jesus's question with, "Yes, Lord, I have always believed you are the Messiah, the Son of God, who has come into the world from God." Martha may have been a slow learner in some areas, but her faith, her encounters with Jesus, and his patience with her brought her to a place of teachability.

Have you ever gotten your priorities confused? I know I have. Has your attention to detail caused you to miss the big picture?

My grandma often told me, "When I've stopped learning, it means I'm dead." How about you? Are you alive and teachable? Are you letting the Spirit of God work in your life to make and keep you teachable? As with Martha, he certainly has been patient with me.

"Teach me how to live, O LORD. Lead me along the right path" (Psalm 27:11 NLT).

Be Disciplined

Discipline. Now there's a word we don't normally like to hear. We like words like freedom, not boundaries. We want what we want, without restrictions. And we think of discipline as an archaic word meaning punishment. It's not for us. After all, we're not bad, are we? Well, are we?

In fact, being disciplined is simply another word for being self-controlled or restrained or well organized. Notice that those synonyms all point inward. Being self-controlled points to the inner self. Being restrained points in. And being well organized begins within before it's seen without.

Being disciplined is a quality that is a must for every leader. It's not necessarily something that we're born with. It's developed.

Even when I was young, I was pretty organized. I managed my time well and could hold my tongue when I thought it was best to do so. But as I mentioned earlier, I had a bit of a rebellious spirit. Sometimes I'd tell myself it wasn't rebellion; it was just healthy stubbornness.

At the Bible school I attended, there was a rule that the women had to wear their skirts or dresses no higher than the middle of their knees. To me, that seemed so outdated. It was the dawn of the miniskirt, and I'd come from a public high school that didn't have such restrictions. Enter my rebellious spirit.

When no one was looking, I'd roll up my skirt, so it was three or four inches above my knees. Seemed reasonable to me. But I knew it was wrong because as soon as I saw someone in authority, I'd roll my skirt back down. Sounds harmless, right? Wrong. It's possible to push the boundaries so that a rebellious attitude develops. An attitude that breeds more rebellion.

The world has seen many significant accomplishments because men and women pushed against injustices that needed to be made right. But when we allow an attitude of rebellion to dictate our hearts, we're not living in the light of God's freedom. We're lost in the darkness of sin. And we are far from living a disciplined life.

Discipline requires action. It's a choice. As leaders, we set goals and order our priorities to achieve those goals. But we must also be mindful of the excuses we give for not sticking to them.

How many times have you intended to complete a project only to get to the end of the day without even looking at it? Or what about a commitment you made to God, but you stumbled and failed, despite your good intentions? Yes, life happens, and something can legitimately pull us away from our best-laid plans. And true, God is a forgiving God.

But how are we being affected by our lack of self-discipline? How is it affecting our spiritual health and leadership vitality? When diversions or failings keep happening, it's time to consider them as excuses. And excuses will only cause us to fail, no matter how self-disciplined we may think we are.

Remember the little song lyric, "Dare to be a Daniel. Dare to stand alone"? Sometimes being disciplined can seem like we're standing alone. Daniel stood alone. Though idolatry surrounded him and he was subject to an egocentric king, he knew above all else that God was sovereign. His commitment to serve God and show leadership in the face of danger required that discipline.

"Look carefully then how you walk, not as unwise but as wise, making the best use of the time, because the days are evil" (Ephesians 5:15–16).

Be Flexible

Years ago, I planned a birthday celebration for my friend Donna. It was a milestone birthday. I pulled out all the stops with a scavenger hunt, leading her through a series of favorite activities for a full weekend. Clues took her from a one-on-one picnic with her daughter to swimming in a private pool, from a candlelight dinner with her husband to a big party with women friends and family, and a relaxing couple of days away for the two of us. The theme of the weekend-long celebration was Expect the Unexpected.

Donna and I often referred to those words as we traveled many miles on vacation or ministry trips together. When I think of being flexible, those same words come to mind—expect the unexpected.

Leadership is full of unexpected twists and turns. Our best plans can change in an instant—someone doesn't show up to follow through on their commitment; there's a family emergency; or a pandemic ravages the world. If we can't learn to be flexible, we will become frustrated—and maybe even give up.

Flexibility is especially critical when working with a team. How we interact with each volunteer or team member demands flexibility. How much time or guidance each person or team requires has to be considered. A unique mix of personalities and gifts may necessitate adjustments for individual growth and group success to be realized. We even see this in our families.

When we're flexible and adapt to changing circumstances and offer accountability, we provide a safe place for individuals to grow and keep going.

Being flexible also involves an attitude of holding our plans lightly. When I draft a plan and present it to a team, I'm quick to remind them it's not set in stone. Anything can happen from day to day—from moment to moment. We need to hold our plans lightly, be ready to change what needs to be changed, and know that God is ultimately in control.

The apostle Paul knew what it was to be flexible. Though he was a free man, he made himself a servant to all. In 1 Corinthians 9:19–22, he tells us how he related to those under the law and those outside the law. How he became weak so he could reach those who were weak. Whether he was alone in prison, sitting with a group of believers, or standing before those who were trying to entrap him, he adapted. But he never deviated from the truth—the plan for which God called him. He was all things to all people so that by all means he might save some.

Be Grounded

The knowledge of who we are in Christ is foundational for every believer and leader. Before we were even a twinkle in our parents' eyes, God had a plan for who we'd become. He created us with certain strengths and gifts to use for his glory. As we mature, those strengths become refined. And as we grow in him, our spiritual gifts also develop.

If you don't know what your strengths or gifts are, talk with people who know you well. Friends and family may see what you can't see for yourself. There are also several assessments available to help identify and understand your strengths and spiritual gifts. As you discover them, don't dismiss your findings. Explore them. Dig into them. Ask God to show you what he wants to reveal.

Being curious, teachable, disciplined, and flexible are all valuable principles for leaders to follow. But above all else, be grounded. Rooted in Scripture, "rightly handling the word of truth" (2 Timothy 2:15). When we're in a difficult situation, headed down a wrong path, or need encouragement, what we've learned comes back to us.

As we become secure in our core beliefs, convictions, and who God created us to be, our relationship with him and his Word becomes solidified. Know the Word. Read it. Absorb it.

Timothy was a young man who became a leader in the early church, but it started at the feet of his mother and grandmother. Eunice and Lois had a solid faith and passed it on to Timothy. We need to not only learn for ourselves but also teach our children and disciple those who look to us for leadership.

When Timothy was older, Paul took him under his wing, picking up where Mom and Grandma had left off. He encouraged him to fan the flame of the gift God had placed in him. In 2 Timothy 1:13–14, Paul told him to hold on to the pattern of wholesome teaching he learned from him, and guard the precious truth entrusted to him. To fulfill what Paul was telling him, Timothy had to ground himself in the truth.

God is the same yesterday, today, and forever. He created each of us—past, present, and future—to achieve his purposes and to glorify him. The question is, are we motivated enough to pass God's faithfulness on to future generations so they can take up where we will one day leave off?

Before we turn to the pages of my story that I once saw as lost years, let me assure you that in God's eyes, nothing is wasted. He redeems and restores all for his glory. He has a common mission for all of us and a unique purpose for each of us. But sometimes that unique purpose takes a detour.

Part 2

WOUNDED BUT HELD

We may walk away from God,
but he never walks away from us.

Collision Course

There's a subtle danger in saying, "I can do this!"
Instead, we need to say, "By the grace of God,
I can do this!"
—Joni Eareckson Tada

Two weeks after I arrived home from the 1984 national conference where I officially became the first president of Women's Ministries of Canada, Jim and I embarked on an adventure we almost missed out on.

Months before, we received an invitation to attend Youth for Christ's International Conference in Hong Kong, followed by the option to tour mainland China for two weeks. This was a dream come true for Jim. Since he first read the book, *Hudson Taylor's Spiritual Secret*, he'd wanted to see China. But this trip seemed impossible. We not only didn't have the funds to go, we also had to consider leaving our nine- and ten-year-old children for a month.

When we started with Youth for Christ, one requirement was to raise 100 percent of our own support. We would receive only what came in each month. When there was a shortfall in any pay period, I learned to make a game out of the shortages we faced. I went through the kitchen cupboards to determine how many more meals I could get out of what we had. When I neared the end of my culinary imagination and the shelves looked close to empty, Jim invariably came home with money that had come through for us. I remember almost being disappointed because I was sure I could have made at least two or three more meals out of what we had. But God knew what we needed, and when we needed it.

While we never went hungry, extras were a luxury, and in our minds, traveling to China fell into the extravagant class. How would the people who contributed financially to our ministry support view such a trip?

It didn't take us long to find out.

One day, a faithful supporter invited us to her office. She was the senior administrator of a local hospital and looked forward to retirement. When we told her of the Hong Kong and China opportunities, she was emphatic. "You need to go."

She then told us of the dream she and her husband had once had to visit the Holy Land and how they agreed to wait until he retired. When his retirement came, they were all set to go when he had a massive heart attack and died. They could never fulfill their dream, and while she eventually took the trip on her own, she lamented, "My biggest regret was that we didn't go earlier. We shouldn't have waited. And neither should you." For emphasis she added, "You need to go to Hong Kong *and* take in the bonus two weeks in China." Reaching across her desk, she reinforced her words with a check to kickstart our China fund.

In a few short months, we raised the money and made plans for our children to be cared for while we were away. With suitcases in tow and limited spending money in our pockets, we said good-bye and boarded a plane. On our overnight layover in California, we called home before flying west toward Asia. In an era of no internet, cell phones, or other convenient ways to connect with family, we knew it would be our last contact until we arrived home a month later.

Having crossed the international dateline, we landed in Hong Kong on July 29, 1984, for a conference unlike any I had ever attended. International speakers and musicians. Representatives from sixty countries. Diverse cultures and foods. A variety of skin colors and accents. A symphony of languages and interpreters with translation equipment. But all with one common denominator—a desire to win young people for Christ.

On our first Sunday, Jim and I boarded a public bus to meet missionary friends on the other side of the city and to attend a local church. Sticky summer air, foreign smells, dirty streets and buildings, and masses of people overwhelmed our senses. As we kept our eyes peeled for landmarks noted in our friends' instructions, we couldn't avoid the constant stares and whispers. We were the only white people around. We didn't know the language. And we hoped we wouldn't need to ask for help.

After arriving at our destination, we walked about six blocks to the church, which was in a building on a busy city street. We made our way to the sixth floor and entered a tiny, crowded room with one small fan to circulate the humid air. We couldn't understand a word but immediately felt at home with these fellow believers. As our missionary friends jotted quick notes to help us know what was being said, we learned the speaker was giving guidance to the small congregation about how to face the impending communist takeover. Another thirteen years would pass before Hong Kong came under the rule of communist China, but there was already a sense of urgency among the people.

As the service drew to a close, I opened the English hymnbook they had handed us when we arrived and turned to the first verse of the closing song. Soon, my eyes filled with tears and my throat tightened as I read the words and listened to the people sing. With unflinching commitment to stay true to Christ no matter what lay ahead, they sang.

> I would be true, for there are those who trust me;
> I would be pure, for there are those who care;
> I would be strong, for there is much to suffer;
> I would be brave, for there is much to dare.[5]

What conviction. What leadership. Faithful Hong Kong Chinese believers boldly stood in the face of an unknown future, to take their stand as a light amid darkness.

Following the end of the conference, we headed into mainland China with twenty-six Youth for Christ supporters. For two weeks, we traveled by bus, train, and plane throughout five provinces. Glimpses of a life we had never known seared their way into our memories. We saw beauty and desolation. Sad sights and touching scenes. Weathered faces with tentative eyes and childlike curiosity.

A few days before we left on our China trip, Grandma's doctor saw something unusual during a regular checkup and wanted her to undergo tests. She wanted to wait until we returned from our trip, but I convinced her to go ahead so the results would be back when we came home a month later.

On August 20, 1984, we arrived home to a bit of culture shock and Grandma's test results. Less than two months later and after more tests, she had her spleen removed. In November, she received the ominous news that she had an uncommon form of leukemia called hairy cell leukemia and Hodgkin's lymphoma—two separate forms of cancer.

True to form, Grandma got back to her responsibilities as soon as she was able. Over the next months, she and I saw myriad doctors, specialists, hospitals, and clinics while we kept up with other commitments. I kept telling myself there was hope—that God was in control and the doctors now knew more about how to treat cancer. Besides, they didn't know my grandma. She was a fighter. Even when sadness filled her life, I saw her stand strong. She'd always been my rock and often told me, "Where there's a will, there's a way." And I believed her.

In April 1985, we rushed Grandma to hospital by ambulance, but she insisted they release her in time for the women's retreat we planned to attend together. She got her wish, but it was to be her last retreat or conference.

Despite the treatments, the disease took hold and wrestled to claim her body as a prize. She became quieter, and I watched the fight drain from her face. Her once healthy body and active mind weakened as each day revealed one more reason to believe our journey together would soon end.

One day, we sat side by side on the couch as I watched her stare quietly across the room and beyond the large picture window. Over the previous couple of weeks, what had once been so effortless for Grandma was now a struggle. Order had become a stranger as overdue notices for unpaid bills showed up in the mail I opened for her. She didn't seem to know where she left things, and I kept finding bits of cash in unusual places. Hesitant to break our quiet moment together, I slowly removed my arm from around her shoulder and turned to face her.

"Grandma, would you like me to do your banking later when I'm out? Or do you need me to mail any bill payments?"

No response.

I persisted. "It's just that I see a couple of late bill notices and thought you'd like me to look after them for you."

A defeated expression came across her face. I felt empty. She seemed to struggle with emotions begging to spill out from her tired body. Slowly, she reached over and picked up her black leather handbag and fumbled with the clasp. Sheer determination won the battle. But as she reached into the bag and felt its contents, I sensed her frustration. I didn't want to pry another piece of independence from her, so I waited until I could wait no longer.

"Grandma, why don't you let me help you?"

When our eyes met, her pride yielded, and she let go of what she always considered private.

As I thumbed through the papers, a heavy weight pushed hard from inside my chest. My heart and mind were fighting against the path they were not yet ready to travel. A thoughtless and malignant intruder had laid claim to the woman who had been my friend, my mentor, my grandma. She, who had always been strong and independent, was now weakened and dependent. At that moment, I realized we were being introduced to a new reality and pushed headlong toward an uninvited future.

Glancing toward Grandma, I saw tears fill her eyes before she did something I had never seen her do before. She laid her head on my shoulder and cried. After a moment, she whispered, "Oh, Ann, what am I going to do?"

I couldn't speak. Tenderly, I held her close and reached up to stroke her soft, thin white hair. She had always comforted and cradled me when my world was less than perfect. Now, as she lay on my shoulder, the tables were turned—upside down and backward.

No matter how bad she felt, I never heard Grandma complain or renege on her commitments. Now, it was time for my commitments to be tested—as a granddaughter and as a leader.

In July, one week after Grandma's eighty-sixth birthday, the doctor admitted her to the hospital so she could regularly receive the pain relief she needed. Three days later, I was expected to leave for a conference almost seven hundred miles away. Months before, Grandma and I had talked about the conference and agreed that I must be there. We didn't, however, expect her health to decline so quickly.

Six years had passed since Grandma encouraged me to get involved with the women of our church, and now my leadership responsibilities stretched across the country. This conference marked the end of the first full year since the inception of Women's Ministries of Canada and my national leadership role. But my mind and heart were a whirlwind of emotions. How could I leave now?

As Grandma slept throughout the day, I sat by her hospital bed working on conference details and presentations. In the early mornings and late evenings, I met with team members and made phone calls while caring for my family, which now included Grandma's two sisters, who had arrived from England.

The day before our family was to leave for the conference, Grandma had a near fall in the hospital, and the nurses restrained her for her own safety. She begged me to help her out of bed, but she was too weak. We delayed our departure by one day, but I couldn't escape a roller coaster of emotions. I didn't want to leave. But as Grandma and I talked briefly about it, we both knew I had to follow through on my commitment. She also expressed her desire for her sisters to go with us so they could see more of the country.

On the morning of our departure, I told her I had arranged for various family and friends to sit with her every day I was gone. I also promised to call my sister twice a day to see how Grandma was doing. Leaning over to kiss her goodbye, I whispered, "Grandma, I'll be back in a week. But I'll drop everything and come home right away if you need me."

Twice a day, I faithfully stole away from conference responsibilities to call for updates. When I phoned my sister at the halfway point of our return trip home, she sounded anxious and told me she'd been waiting for my call.

"Come right away," she said. "Grandma's not doing well."

Within hours, my husband dropped me off at the hospital

before taking everyone home and unloading our VW bus. After rushing through the automatic doors, I took the elevator to Grandma's floor and made my way toward her room. My heart jumped at the sight of other family members standing in the hallway outside her room, and a sick feeling overcame me. *Am I too late?* Hoping no one would make a fuss about my arrival, I paused at the door, drew in a deep breath, and stepped into the room.

"Grandma, Ann's here," my sister said as she leaned over Grandma's bed.

Grandma turned her head, and a gentle but strained smile welcomed me. I cupped her face in my hands and bent down to kiss her.

Softly, but loud enough for all to hear, she said, "That's my girl. Everything's okay now."

Everyone in the room looked at each other with shocked expressions and my sister said, "Those are the first words any of us have heard her speak since you left a week ago."

Though she was obviously tired, Grandma managed a weak smile for each family member when they trickled into the room to kiss her before leaving as quietly as they arrived.

After the last goodbyes, it didn't take the nurses long to realize I wasn't moving from Grandma's side. When she closed her eyes, I was there. When she opened them, she looked at me, smiled, and squeezed my hand. I knew she wanted me there. And I wasn't about to leave.

After a week of my sleeping on a chair by Grandma's bed, the nurses brought me a cot and bedding so I could lie down at night. But sleep was difficult as Grandma's pain increased, and she struggled to breathe.

Each day, I sat and tried to write or read. Sometimes I read out loud. Sometimes I simply leaned over and rested my head on her bed. When friends or family came to visit, I went to the visitors lounge or walked up and down the hall. Periodically, I left the hospital, walked to my home a block away, took a quick shower, and rushed back.

As the first week passed into the second, Grandma's breathing became more labored. Even the patients and visitors in the hallway could hear her struggle between this world and the next. One evening near the end of that second week, a nurse came to check on us. When she turned to leave, I looked up and said, "Thank you for what you're doing for my grandma."

The nurse paused, gazed at me intently, and said, "Ann, we can't say when someone is going to pass away, but," she whispered, "I don't think you should be alone tonight."

When she left the room, I looked at Grandma's face and held her soft, swollen hand. The reality was setting in. These were likely our last hours together. Stepping to the payphone in the hallway outside Grandma's room, I called my friend and mentor, Eileen Enarson. She had been our only visitor that day and had just arrived home.

I didn't have to say much before she said, "I'll be right there."

Throughout the night, we took turns on the cot while each breath forced another bit of life into Grandma's body.

Just before six o'clock on the morning of Tuesday, August 13, 1985, I jumped from the cot when Grandma's breathing suddenly changed. During long waits between breaths, my mind coaxed her to take another breath.

When she took her last gasp and there was no more breathing to mix with my tears, Eileen whispered, "I'm going to get the nurse, Ann."

"No, not yet." I choked. I didn't want anyone to come between me and my grandma.

For a few more moments, Eileen and I stood in silence. No talking. No breathing. No gasping. Just quiet tears.

"Ann, I really need to get the nurse now," Eileen whispered again. I knew she was right and gave a slight nod.

When she left the room, I only heard my own muffled sobs. I gazed at Grandma lying peaceful and still. There was no more struggle. No more pain. No more breath. I wanted to bend over and kiss her, but told myself that when I did, it would be final—the end. She would be gone.

As I stood there with her hand in mine and stroked her soft white hair, I had the overwhelming sense I was not alone. That Grandma was still in the room. Her presence was there, and we were having our last moments together. In the silence, I felt her arms around me, comforting and encouraging me.

In the past, we were there for one another. We loved each other through good and bad. Now, time suspended us in that moment—an intimate gift reserved for the two of us. Then, as if on cue, I leaned over, held Grandma close, and kissed her gently. It was time.

"Bye, Grandma. I love you. See you later," I whispered.

And my world stood still.

 — Selah —

Grandma's death changed my world, and it changed my life. I no longer had her wisdom to lean on or her unconditional love to enfold me. I no longer could ask her about this or that or draw on her talents. Time had run out on our shopping sprees and talks over lunch. I now had to adjust to my new reality—a reality that ruthlessly dogged my every waking moment.

Comments like "she's in a better place now" or "she made such a difference and will be missed by so many" were well intentioned but didn't ease the pain. They only made the hole feel bigger.

Before Grandma's cancer diagnosis, I rode waves of mountain-top experiences. During her brief, one-year illness, the two of us faced her deadly intruder together while I kept up with my own little family and hectic schedule.

When she died, sorrow cast me into an abyss of grief. But rather than take time and stand toe-to-toe with my profound loss to work through it, I ran. I ran into a world of *more*. More speaking engagements. More leadership roles. Lots of busyness and responsibilities. More. More. More.

What I didn't do was take time to rest—to sleep, to contemplate, to gather myself physically, emotionally, mentally, and spiritually. I didn't listen to that still, small voice that said, *Come away and rest a while.*

In 1 Kings 17, we read of the prophet Elijah going head-to-head with ruthless King Ahab, who did more evil in the eyes of God than any king before him. Scripture presents Elijah as a man with a feisty demeanor and a take-no-prisoners commitment to the God of Israel. He was a bold man who did not hesitate to deliver the messages God gave him to speak.

When he first confronted King Ahab, his confident words spoke with authority. "As the Lord the God of Israel lives, before whom I stand, there shall be neither dew nor rain these years, except by my word" (1 Kings 17:1).

Can you imagine what people must have thought at that moment? *Uh-oh, Elijah's done it now. The king won't take this one lying down. And knowing Elijah, he won't back off either. Better get ready for a fight.*

One would almost expect the showdown we see later in 1 Kings 18. There, Elijah challenges the prophets of Baal and shows them the power of the one true God who controls fire, rain, and everything else.

But not this time. Once Elijah delivered God's message to King Ahab, God didn't tell him to stand his ground and get ready for a fight. Instead, he gave Elijah what may seem like an unusual battle strategy.

In essence, God said, *Go away and hide yourself by the brook, Cherith. While you're there, I'll take care of getting food and water for you. But for now, all I want you to do is rest.*

Elijah may have been ready to get busy in the fight, but God knew he needed to rest and gain strength for even bigger battles that lay ahead.

How many times do we throw ourselves into busyness when what we really need is rest? Time to come away from all demands so we can grieve. Time to draw on God's wisdom and strength for our next steps. And time to simply *be.*

A lot about the weeks and months during and after Grandma's graduation to heaven are a blur to me. But as the years passed and I gained a bit more maturity, I came to understand that her passing had affected me far more than I realized. Throwing myself into activity took its toll and led me to the edge of a wilderness.

Cracks in the Foundation

*Deep hurts, resulting in spiritual scar tissue,
have their own sinister way of impeding our progress.*
—Eileen Enarson

When passion takes hold, it can catapult us into joy and fulfill-
ment or plunge us into despair and defeat.

As I scan the pieces I wrote and talks I gave over the two years
following Grandma's passing, it's clear I was passionate about the
work God had entrusted to me. I dove into activities that were
all good—organizing major events, encouraging women, teaching,
writing, and more. In retrospect, I believe I was in the center of
God's will and plan for my life. But were all my activities the best
of what God wanted for me? Was I fully listening to him, or was
self-interest creeping in?

One good, and maybe even best, undertaking happened when
Vancouver, Canada, hosted World Expo '86. A contagious buzz
grew as Vancouver became the place to be.

Leading up to the big event, a group of Christians had the
vision to reach millions of visitors with the gospel. Together, they
launched HOPE '86, with the overarching goal of reaching the

world for Christ. Many Christian organizations and churches came together to host venues all over the greater Vancouver area and provide a variety of outreach events throughout the city.

The central flagship became the Pavilion of Promise, on the main grounds and among other pavilions from around the world. Though there was initially some opposition to anything other than an interfaith pavilion, the decision-makers finally gave their approval. Through multimedia, some 750,000 Expo visitors witnessed a presentation on the life, death, and resurrection of Christ. In the end, HOPE '86 became an evangelistic endeavor like no other we had ever witnessed.

As part of this huge undertaking, a Women's Task Force came together to reach women across all walks of life. It was my honor and privilege to be selected to chair a first-rate group of women leaders from various organizations, denominations, and backgrounds. When we first met together, most of us didn't know each other, but we were ready to roll up our sleeves and work as a team.

I later learned that during our first meeting there were people outside the boardroom who were both curious and dubious. They had doubts that a group of women from diverse backgrounds and doctrinal convictions could work together. They expected the venture to dissolve before we got anything off the ground—even our inaugural meeting. But this amazing team of nineteen women leaders focused on reaching women for Christ and seeing them grow where God placed them. The energetic initiatives we undertook extended to women serving in business, home, politics, and ministry roles. In the end, God accomplished the purposes and goals he helped us establish at that first meeting.

But all "good" is not necessarily all "best."

God placed within me a specific passion that I dedicated myself to fulfilling. Life was full of good activities—studying, preparing Bible studies and presentations, and organizing teams for events.

Talks I gave spoke a lot about commitment, being a woman with purpose, and what to do when the going gets tough. Women were being inspired to commit themselves to the Lord and serve him where they were. It was an invigorating time of "doing"—until everything came to a screeching halt.

I brought my car to a full stop behind the vehicle in front of me because another car up ahead was waiting to turn. As I glanced at my rearview mirror, I saw a big old boat of a car coming down the hill behind me and gaining speed. In seconds, there was a loud crash and my Volkswagen bus saw its last day.

When the ambulance delivered me to the hospital, I was told, "You must lie still. Don't make a move."

All I could think about was that I was going to be late for a meeting. If the nurses and doctors would hurry, I could still make it. But as the hours crept by and nurses bustled around, I could only continue to look up at the ceiling.

Why, Lord? You know I have a speaking trip in two days and there's a lot to do before I leave. Why did this have to happen now? Then I chuckled when I remembered the topic the organizers had asked me to speak on in a couple of days—patience.

But Lord, I didn't think I needed another illustration.

Sometimes we are so passionate about what we're doing that we neglect to stop and listen to God's still, small voice. We become blind to the simple lessons he tries to show us within the circumstances of the day or through the wisdom of people he puts in our lives.

As my leadership roles with HOPE '86 and the national women's ministries drew to their completion, I wondered what was next. Travel, working with amazing teams, and interacting with a cross section of women, had exposed me to a broad scope of needs. I had learned so much, wanted to keep going, and thought the local church was the place to accomplish it.

But while my vision and passion were growing, I was also experiencing some open opposition to what I saw as possibilities for women reaching women through the church. I heard remarks like, "There is no need for women's ministries" or "If Christian women are involved in ministry, they will have no needs to be addressed." These and other comments led me to believe that my personal involvement in church ministry was about to become drastically limited.

Over the years, an extremely effective ministry to women had grown exponentially at my home church. But something had changed. Church leadership no longer seemed to support the creative development of a well-thought-through ministry to and for women, administered by women.

If I implemented even a limited part of what I believed was a viable plan for women reaching women through the church, I risked appearing to oppose the leadership of the church. That was something I was not willing to do. Further, if I pursued the issue, it could jeopardize the future of any women's ministries. Again, I was not prepared to do that. I also felt that the potential for misunderstood intentions was very high and did not want to cause any kind of division.

I presented a written proposal for consideration on how we might move forward but didn't receive the opportunity to meet with church leadership to talk about it. They simply read, discussed, and rejected it. With sadness, I ended all my church leadership involvement.

Someone once asked me, "What is your greatest frustration in women's ministries?"

My reply was simply, "The work that still needs to be done." My concerns for any ministry to women was that it would deteriorate into nothing more than a sterile social clique. And I believed God intended it to be much more.

One of my journal entries from that time read:

God help us if we ever become so satisfied with how far we've come that we lose sight of how much further we must still go. Standing still will only cause us to lose ground and slide backward while Satan marches forward, claiming territory that belongs to God.

So, now what? Where do I go from here? I had fulfilled a three-year national commitment and, according to the rules, passed the baton to the next board. I had successfully completed my role in HOPE '86. And the doors had closed on what could have been a broader local church ministry.

Questions hit me like a battering ram repeatedly colliding with its intended victim. If I wasn't doing those things, who was I? What was I here for? Did I fail somehow? Does God not want me anymore? Where could I now focus my energies and passion?

I wonder if Moses asked those questions when he fled from Egypt and into the desert.

We now know that Moses's destiny was to be one of the greatest leaders of the people of Israel. But when he was a young man, that wasn't completely evident. He spent his early years with his God-fearing family, learning the ways of the God of Israel. At a young age, they took him to the palace where Pharaoh's daughter raised him as part of the ruling family of Egypt.

According to the historian Josephus, Pharaoh had no son and heir. Therefore, it makes sense that Moses, Pharaoh's adopted grandson, had the greatest minds of Egypt tutor and groom him for the day he would sit on the Egyptian throne. His education would have included the ancient Egyptian hieroglyphic language and all the disciplines of the time—from medicine, astronomy, chemistry, and other known sciences to philosophy, the law, military strategies, and the arts.

"And Moses was instructed in all the wisdom of the Egyptians, and he was mighty in his words and deeds" (Acts 7:22).

Here was a charismatic and educated man who accomplished all he set his mind to. He was intelligent, respected, and influential. Extrabiblical historians also considered him a brilliant military leader who led the Egyptian army to victories over their enemies.

One day, after a few years had passed, Moses went for a walk and saw the extensive hardship endured by the Israelites. Though Moses was now forty years of age and had spent most of his life being educated in the ways of Egypt, it's clear he knew the Israelites were his people. He had not forgotten where he came from or what he learned from his Israelite parents. He knew who he was. "When he was forty years old, it came into his heart to visit his brothers, the children of Israel" (Acts 7:23).

It also seems apparent that Moses knew God intended him to deliver the Israelites out of their bondage. The question was, "When?" When he saw an Egyptian beating an Israelite, he knew he had to do something. He also believed his fellow Israelites would know he was there for them.

"And seeing one of them being wronged, he defended the oppressed man and avenged him by striking down the Egyptian. He supposed that his brothers would understand that God was giving them salvation by his hand, but they did not understand" (Acts 7:24–25).

Were Moses's actions a bad thing, a good thing, or a best thing? Was this God's plan or Moses's plan? I believe Moses knew that what he was doing was wrong. Exodus 2:12 tells us that before he hit the Egyptian, "he looked this way and that, and seeing no one, he struck down the Egyptian and hid him in the sand."

Moses didn't look up and ask God for direction by saying,

"Holy God of Israel, what do you want me to do? What is your best?" Instead, he looked around to see if anyone was looking. Was he angry at what he witnessed? Did he feel justified in coming to the rescue of one of his own people? Either way, there seems to be no doubt he knew that what he was about to do was wrong.

Did Moses know God was going to use him to deliver his people, but then went against God's timing? Did he take matters into his own hands before waiting for God to say, *Okay, Moses, now's the right time to free my people from slavery.*

It appears he soon realized he was in the wrong because the next day when he saw two Israelites arguing and tried to break up the fight, they confronted him with hostility. "Who made you a ruler and a judge over us? Do you want to kill me as you killed the Egyptian yesterday?" (Acts 7:27–28).

At that point, Moses became afraid. He didn't seem to belong anywhere. The Israelites didn't support him coming to their friend's rescue when he was being beaten, and they didn't appreciate him interfering in their affairs. Even Pharaoh turned against him, and the army he once led was now out to get him. "When Pharaoh heard of it, he sought to kill Moses" (Exodus 2:15).

And Moses fled. He was no longer at home in Pharaoh's courts and certainly wasn't welcome among his own people, the Israelites. No home. No family. And no focus. Where did he belong? What was he supposed to do?

So, what did he do? He ran to Midian—a desolate place. A hot and dry desert land with nothing but sand, gravel, and rock peppered with scraggly bushes clinging to life itself. Imagine it. Moses knew God had a noble purpose for him, but he ran when he hit a bump in the road.

Did he plan to run to the desert? Maybe not. Was he thinking about where he was going? Probably not. He was just a man dressed in royal clothes with nowhere to turn. He was a man on the run.

When he finally stopped running long enough to sit by a well to be refreshed, God put him in the position of again coming to someone's rescue. I wonder what went through his mind at that moment. *Once bitten, twice shy. Do I step in and help? I'm a stranger here. Maybe I shouldn't interfere. Look where it got me last time.*

But, Moses being Moses, he stuck his neck out to help someone being mistreated and came to the rescue of women being harassed by some shepherds. When they later told their father about the man who helped them, they described him as an Egyptian. "An Egyptian delivered us out of the hand of the shepherds and even drew water for us and watered the flock" (Exodus 2:19).

We see Moses stripped of all that identified him as an Israelite. His clothing revealed him to be an Egyptian. He was now a wanderer in a parched desert, homeless, and far from his palatial home. Rather than enjoying the company of many friends, he now confronted strangers at a well in the middle of the desert. The once-revered prince of a great nation became the lowly shepherd of someone else's flock. But he was still God's man.

Moses experienced rejection. He struggled with who he was and what he would do next. But, in years to come, he learned that no matter where he went or what he did, God's everlasting arms were there (Deuteronomy 33:27), and he could always take refuge in the shadow of his wings (Psalm 36:7).

It turns out that the rejection and struggle period in my life affected me beyond what I could have imagined. As I dug into my personal papers to help recall details of that time, I came across a card I received from my mentor, Eileen Enarson. I don't know why I kept it, but I'm glad I did. It holds so much wisdom that settles my heart even now.

These past months have been exceedingly difficult for you. Many, many prayers have gone to the throne

of God as hearts have interceded for you. Only the Lord himself can lighten your burden and brighten your pathway . . . As one of Jehovah's very own, very special children, you will use this milestone not as a stumbling stone but as a stepping-stone. And all the way, in the time he allots to you, there will be fruit for his glory from the valley experiences wherein those stones have appeared.

Inasmuch as my heart's desire has been, and is, to do what I can to lift the Savior and bring honor to his name, I trust him to give me wisdom to not attempt to do the things I cannot. Deep hurts, resulting in spiritual scar tissue, have their own sinister way of impeding our progress. Wisdom applied with dispatch may prevent some of those experiences.

On the other hand, our loving heavenly Father knows what we need, and also what others need because of and through us, that he sovereignly sends us situations—always for our good (Jeremiah 29:11)—that prune us so that we might bear more fruit for him!

Milestone. Stumbling stone. Stepping-stone. "Fruit for his glory from the valley experiences wherein those stones have appeared." Oh, my goodness. If only I had seen the wisdom in those words back then. But God . . .

I was about to become lost in a desert wilderness, blinded by the "deep hurts resulting in spiritual scar tissue" that would make lasting marks on my life. But God . . .

Though I was about to walk away from everything I knew to be true, and the passion for ministry God placed in my being, my heart for women remained. But God . . .

The Great Escape

God seldom intervened when people
were about to make mistakes.
Rather, he allowed them to fail,
but stood ready to redeem them.
—Henry and Richard Blackaby

When ministry commitments drew to a close, I felt dismissed. I'd served faithfully and with all my being. Yet I was left wondering, what do I do now? My family had sacrificed so I could travel and spend hours to prepare for all my involvements. Yet how did their sacrifice affect anything? Did any of it really matter at all?

I felt like Moses, wandering around in the desert—no place to go, no one to turn to, and nothing to focus on. My world was about to spiral out of control, and I couldn't seem to stop it.

God, where are you?

Despite my sense of loss, I kept somewhat busy with family while coordinating contractors for the house we were building. When it was complete, we moved into our new home, and I took on the role of screening and managing renters for both sides of the duplex we had previously shared with Grandma. Yet nothing seemed to fill the void I felt deep inside. I was a wanderer in the desert.

Amid my continuing sense of ministry loss, Jim was fully engaged in his work with Youth for Christ. He was invited to undertake broader leadership roles but expressed apprehension. Youth for Christ asked us to consider moving to either Montreal, Quebec, or Manila, Philippines. But as we prayed about both opportunities, we came to believe it was not wise to thrust our budding teenage children into unfamiliar cultures and languages and away from all they knew.

With that decision behind us, I remember sitting in our kitchen and hearing Jim ask, "If something happened to me, what would you do to provide for you and the kids?"

Wow—what a question. I was thirty-seven years old and hadn't even considered that possibility. You'd think my first response would be, "God will take care of us." But it wasn't. And the first threads of the life I knew began to unravel.

As I thought about Jim's question, I wondered what I could do to earn a living. It was an era when churches rarely employed women to their ministry staff, and I couldn't see myself waiting tables at a restaurant. I researched different career alternatives and took a preliminary real estate exam to determine if that was a viable option. I passed with flying colors but decided it wasn't the way to go. Now what?

When a continuing education catalog arrived at our door, I leafed through the pages and came to the business section. Some of the course descriptions intrigued me, but when I landed at a local college that offered Marketing 101, I stopped. *Hmmm—that looks interesting.* I didn't fully understand it, but I've never been shy about being stretched.

After Bible school, my early college education had been in law enforcement and social sciences. Marketing would be different, but

I was ready for something new. I applied and was accepted into an evening class of mature students who were mostly my age and older—business and professional people broadening their education to climb the corporate ladder. The professor was an experienced business owner. He had also taught for several years and was still active in business.

Every day between classes, I put in extra time trying to understand what I was reading and make sense of the homework. The terminology was foreign to me; the scenarios discussed in class were unfamiliar, and I struggled to relate in an environment so different from what I knew. What on earth was I doing there?

After three or four weeks of poring over concepts and struggling to grasp their relevance, I sat in our kitchen with books and papers blanketing the table. I memorized definitions, but what sense did they make in the full scheme of things? How did the words connect to the situations my classmates described? As my eyes blurred over the words, a light suddenly went on in my mind.

"I know this," I said out loud to no one. "The textbook and professor are teaching strategic planning principles."

What I was trying to understand in the course content was what God had previously revealed to me and I'd used in my ministry years. The terminology was different, but the concepts were the same. It couldn't be that simple.

That night during a class break, I talked with the professor. I wanted to be sure what I thought I'd discovered was what he was actually teaching. I was right. Finally, I understood what this marketing stuff was about.

From that point on, I excelled in the class and could take part in discussions. As the course drew to a close, the professor approached me.

"You know, you really should go into business for yourself."

"What? Me? No. I have no experience to speak of and have only taken this one marketing course."

"But you could do it. You're a leader and a fast learner."

"I don't think so. There's so much more to learn before I do anything like that. I wouldn't even know where to start?"

"That's the typical response of a woman," he shot back.

What? Did he just say that? "What do you mean?" I asked.

"Well, a man rallies to the challenge and plows ahead, regardless of the mistakes he makes along the way. But women hold back. They wait until they're sure they have everything in order. Meanwhile, opportunities pass them by."

I went home that night knowing I was not one to be afraid of a challenge. But the words I'd heard from my professor took me back—"That's the typical response of a woman." Had he just thrown down a gauntlet I was being goaded into picking up? Or was I being pushed in a new life direction? I believed I'd hit the ceiling of church leadership while the business world appeared to offer limitless opportunities.

I didn't know which way to turn. Sadly, I didn't seek God's wisdom for direction. If I had, I may never have chomped down hard on the bait dangling from an enticing line.

Within a couple of months, I'd officially registered my new business venture and set up shop with a phone and borrowed desk in the backroom of a friend's group of offices. Years of experience working in ministry and not-for-profit organizations prompted me to focus on providing marketing services to that sector. After all, hadn't I learned in class to go with what we know?

During the first year, I educated myself by reading business publications, engaging with business organizations, and developing relationships with people who helped me along the way. I convinced prospective clients I could provide the work they needed and delivered on my promise. Small-business owners soon noticed what I was doing for not-for-profits and asked if I could do the same for them. I had realized I would be a nonprofit business if I worked only for not-for-profit clients, so I agreed.

The business soon expanded into its own suite of offices, more clients came onboard, and I hired staff to meet the growing demand. Developing something from the ground up and building a cohesive team was what I reveled in. As I became involved in the local business community, I made a good name for myself and believed I was accomplishing something that made a difference. But was I?

Somewhere along the line, I began letting go of the biblical principles built into my life. I put up a good front with Christian friends but frequented places I knew I didn't belong. I'd be in the office from early morning until late at night. And I'd often end the day by going out for a nightcap with new friends. I spent very little time at home.

With the help of my team of designers and support staff, we met all work commitments. However, my health suffered, and I was running into financial difficulties. Determined not to short-change my loyal staff, I borrowed from friends and drew against credit cards to meet payroll and pay overdue invoices.

Surprisingly, I continued playing drums at church for special occasions. One evening, I sat at the drum kit behind the rest of the band. We were playing for a special drama and music presentation, but I knew I was just going through the motions. I looked out across the filled-to-capacity auditorium and into the faces of many people whom I'd known since I was a young girl. They had watched me grow up and take on leadership roles but had no idea what was now going on in my life.

My heart was breaking. My body ached. And my head debated over right and wrong. My life was a lie. I'd enjoyed playing drums most of my life. It had become worship for me. But that too was now a lie. Sadly, that event was the last time I played until many years later.

Church became history, and church friends faded away. I questioned everything I knew to be true about God and the relationship we once enjoyed. He was no longer part of my decision-making process. Although I gained friends and some good advice along the way, I also listened to ungodly and unwise counsel, and interacted with people who didn't always have my best interests at heart. A vortex of drinking and activities pulled me further and further away from God. A tug-of-war raged between the godly life I knew with my family and the ungodly existence that I allowed to yank me away from them.

What was wrong with me?

On the home front, Jim had left Youth for Christ and was struggling to settle on a job. Our children were full-blown teenagers, and our marriage was not doing well. My work consumed all my time and home life suffered. As pressure mounted, the borrowing I convinced Jim to make against our personal assets contributed a great deal to the precarious position our family was in.

After consulting with Realtors, we made the agonizing decision to sell the home we'd built, and move back into one side of our duplex while renting out the other side. It felt like a step backward, but I wanted to focus on the future. Jim was near tears as the movers drove away and we stood quietly alone—together in the center of our empty dream house.

We hoped the move would help remedy some of our personal financial shortfalls. At the same time, advisers told me to close my company and walk away so I could start up again with a clean slate.

"Everyone does it." The advisers rationalized. "By law, you're not personally liable for the company's outstanding debts."

But something inside me whispered, "It's not right. You can't just walk away and leave people hanging. Clients disappeared without paying for what they owed you. What did that do to your business? Honor God and follow through on your commitments."

As I pored over the pros and cons of three viable alternatives, none jumped off the paper and said, "I'm your best option." The stress level was over the top. Was it pride that blinded me to the reality that the advice I was getting wasn't the best advice? Was it pride that kept driving me to keep going despite the dark clouds? Did pride fade God from the picture of my life so that I didn't think to turn to him when I needed him most?

Then the answer came. One morning in 1991, the very talented graphic designer who was the first person I'd hired and now led our creative department came to me with an idea. After running the plan by my lawyer and accountant, we set out to close the existing business and open under a new name.

However, rather than walk away from the tens of thousands of dollars owed to suppliers, we sent them what we called Smart Dollars. These were time-limited vouchers for one hundred percent of money owed to them. They could cash them in for creative or strategic work we would provide. My staff and I would work weekends and evenings to pay off the former company's debt, while building up a new company under a different name.

The result was amazing. Staff rallied to the cause. Ninety-five percent of our suppliers accepted our offer and also continued to support the new company. The business community applauded our creative solution, complete with a glowing business magazine article that came out a year later, recounting what we had accomplished.[6]

When I moved the new business to office space closer to the hub of the city, I took on larger clients and changed from a staff-driven business model to a dynamic contract team approach. This made more financial sense and allowed for greater flexibility. Rather than paying year-round salaries when work was slow, I pulled together a team of talented design, media, public relations, and promotions people who were available as work came in. The result was a loyal group of contractors who had their own independent boutique businesses but came together to service clients I brought to the table. Again, I was doing what I enjoyed—developing something new and building a cohesive team.

But all was not as it appeared. The business was doing well despite the typical ebbs and flows of challenges and accomplishments that accompany any business venture. But a secret was about to be exposed and threatened to bring everything crashing down.

After work one night in January 1992, Jim and I met for dinner at a local restaurant. While we waited for our order to arrive, he turned to me and asked a pointed question about someone I'd been spending a lot of time with. Horrified, I sat stunned but couldn't deny it. He then told me he had talked with our pastor about it, as well as with our two teenage children. I was beyond horrified. This was a personal matter. Why hadn't he talked with me first?

My face turned red with anger. My body shook with embarrassment. I felt hot and cold all at the same time. My brain seemed incapable of getting messages to my lips so they could say something, anything. I sat at the table, frozen in time, oblivious to anything or anyone in the room. The emotion was boiling up inside me and I knew I was about to explode. *Get out now!* My inner voice shouted.

Reaching for my keys, I blurted, "I have to go. I have to go."

"Where are you going?"

"I don't know. I just have to go—now."

My mind was numb with pain. My shattered heart cried out. And my body didn't care what happened. I got into my car and turned the key in the ignition, just as pent-up emotions unleashed themselves from deep within me. I drove through busy streets and onto the main highway where the car hit speeds no vehicle should ever reach on a public road.

A full-blown war raged. Injured pride stood armed for battle. Fear of loss shouted its defense. And embarrassment poised itself for judgment.

Before I knew it, I realized I was heading straight to the person and relationship that had been a secret—until now. Then, in stark contrast and without thinking, I steered off the highway and toward my longtime, trusted girlfriend.

Stopping in front of Bev's house, I waited. Not knowing who might be home, I took deep breaths to compose myself before walking up the sidewalk to the front door. When the door opened, I heard Bev's cheerful voice.

"Hi. What a pleasant surprise."

No words. My face said it all. And another round of emotions erupted. Bev was alone at home and dropped everything to focus on me. She watched me pace the floor, cry, blurt out words that probably made little sense, pace, and cry some more. Finally, in sheer exhaustion, I dropped to the floor while Bev sat silently on the couch beside me.

"Yes, she's here and okay," I heard her say when she answered the phone. "She'll stay with me tonight."

As hours passed, Bev knew I needed to sleep. She also knew there was something else I first needed to do.

"Despite everything that's gone on, you feel betrayed," Bev began. "You believe Jim was wrong to go to the pastor with his suspicions and to reveal it all to your kids, right?"

"Yes," I muttered.

"Okay then. Before you go to bed, I want to hear you say you forgive him."

My mind was a blur. How could she ask me to do what felt impossible?

After a long silence and many attempts to make my heart, head, and lips connect, I finally blurted, "I forgive Jim." It was one of the hardest things I ever did, probably because I knew I was wrong and needed forgiveness.

The next day, I rallied all the inner courage I could find to return home. I didn't know what the future held, but I knew I first had to face Jim and our teenagers. As I drove into our driveway, I did not know what to expect. Slowly, I climbed out of my red 280 ZX T-top sports car, walked a few steps to the front door, stepped into the house, and stood at the bottom of the stairs. Taking a deep breath, I took a couple of slow, deliberate steps up the staircase before hearing my seventeen-year-old daughter's tender and discerning voice.

"Hi, Mom. Are you okay?"

Sarah stood quietly while I trudged to the top of the staircase and into her outstretched arms. The warmth and acceptance in her loving embrace melted my heart. It was one of the first steps in my long journey back from the great escape that had taken me into a desert place.

Later that day, I thought about all that had happened and considered the multiple calls and messages I received urging me to run away with the now not-so-secret person on the other end of the calls. An inner war escalated as I made one of the most important decisions of my life. In that moment, alone in my bedroom, I knew I had to stay and face whatever lay ahead. I couldn't walk away from our children or the vows I'd made twenty years earlier. For better. For worse. For richer. For poorer. In sickness and in health. Till death do us part. It would be a long and hard road back—but it was a start.

When Jonah ran from God, God did not run from Jonah. When Ann ran from God, God did not run from Ann. When you run from God, God does not run from you.

If you stop reading the story of Jonah at the point where a big fish swallows him up, you would miss out on some of the greatest mysteries of God's restorative grace and boundless love. If you stop reading this book and dismiss its words because the author experienced a wilderness journey that led to failure and sin, you'd miss out on some of the greatest mysteries of God's restorative grace and boundless love. You'd also miss out on God's compassion and mercy that says no one is beyond redemption. He loves each of us, even when we fail.

When Jonah ran, he may have thought God had abandoned him. But God was there. When a storm threatened the boat Jonah was on and he told the sailors to save themselves by throwing him overboard, God was there. As Jonah took his final drowning gasps before a great fish swallowed him up, God was there. And, yes, even while Jonah languished in the fish's belly and cried out to God in despair, believing he was at the end of his life, God was there.

> In my distress I called to the LORD, and he answered me. From the deep in the realm of the dead, I called for help and you listened to my cry. You hurled me into the depths, into the very heart of the seas, and the currents swirled about me; all your waves and breakers swept over me. I said, "I have been banished from your sight; yet I will look again toward your holy temple." The engulfing waters threatened me, the deep surrounded me; seaweed was wrapped around my head. To the roots of the mountains, I sank down; the earth beneath barred me in forever. But you, LORD my God, brought my life up from the pit. (Jonah 2:2–6, NIV)

Our wilderness may be great, but God is greater. We may run or try to escape, but God is there. We may get overwhelmed and swallowed up, but God is mightier. And we may think there is nothing left to live for, but God knows more.

I was about to embark on a long and difficult road.
But God . . .

Running from Leadership

*For each of us—no matter what our situation
or how we feel we have failed—there is hope.*
—Catherine Marshall

As we come to the close of this second section, Wounded but Held, I'm well aware that the previous chapters were difficult for some of you to read. Believe me, they weren't easy to write. More than once, I threw up my hands and groaned, "I can't write this. It happened so long ago. Why rehash all the pain and hurt? I just want it left behind." But each time I felt tempted to abandon the writing, my hands fell back to the keyboard and God whispered in my ear, *It's okay, Ann. I got ya. Now write.*

We all have skeletons in our closets that we'd much rather leave buried forever. But sometimes those skeletons need to be unearthed so their stories can bring encouragement, healing, and hope to others. So . . . I write.

When we run from leadership, we're not just running from God's call on our lives, we're running from God himself. Look at Moses, Jonah, David, and Naomi, to name only four biblical characters who ran. Each individual escaped to what became their wilderness—the desert and a foreign way of life, the sea and near-death by drowning, deceit and murder to cover up adultery, grief and bitterness under a new name. In their own way, each had their unique wilderness. Each one ran from God. But God did not run from them. In each experience, God was there. And eventually, each individual fulfilled God's greater plan.

Someone once asked me, "What was it that plunged you into your wilderness years?"

I thought for a moment and replied, "I really don't know. No one ever asked me that before." But that question got me thinking deeper.

Without a doubt, we can wander slowly into a wilderness. We make one poor decision, or someone makes an inappropriate comment that throws us off. We make a wrong turn, and before we know it, missteps compound into another wrong decision or unfortunate comment or misguided detour. And so it goes until we beat ourselves up and wonder how on earth we ended up in such a miserable place.

Yes, it's possible to identify something major that caused us to turn our back on God and/or the church. But I believe it's more likely an accumulation of words, decisions, and/or actions. Each one can play a supporting role we suppress or ignore, until that one event puts us over the edge and we declare, "I'm outta here."

So, how can we shield ourselves from taking an ill-fated journey into a wilderness and down a road of regret? How can we guard against an adversary who prowls around like a roaring lion, looking for someone to devour (1 Peter 5:8)? How can we smother the flaming darts before they hit us (Ephesians 6:16)?

This chapter could become a dissertation on how to stay on the straight and narrow or in the center of God's plan for your life. It could provide multiple Scripture passages in the footnotes. However, for our time here, I'd like to highlight four principles I painfully realized as I rehearsed my wilderness story and studied the wanderings of biblical characters who could teach us volumes about running from God and leadership.

Beware of Misdirected Pride

History recounts the story of a self-made man who began as a hired hand on a farm in Kansas. By sheer determination, he worked his way up and amassed a considerable fortune. When his wife died, John Davis hired a sculptor in Italy to design an elaborate statue in her memory.

He was so pleased with the monument, which showed both him and his wife at opposite ends of a love seat, that he commissioned another statue. This time it was of himself kneeling and placing a wreath at her grave. That, too, impressed him so much that he planned a third monument. This time, the statue was of his wife kneeling and placing a wreath at his future gravesite.

One idea led to another until he spent up to an estimated one million dollars on eleven life-size marble monuments to himself and his wife. He had also erected a granite slab on six granite pillars over the Davis plot and surrounded it with a three-foot high granite wall. Meanwhile, the town was suffering in the depths of the Great Depression of the 1930s. Whenever someone suggested he might contribute to a community project such as a hospital or park for the children, the old miser's response was that it was his money and he would spend it the way he wanted.

It appears John Davis, who had no children and who people viewed as a cantankerous and crotchety old man, didn't see the needs of those around him. Rather than use his wealth to help build facilities to benefit the town for generations, he erected stone monuments that focused on himself. His misdirected pride alienated everyone.[7]

Our pride can send us down a path, away from God's best for our lives. We choose to do something a certain way, sometimes knowing that it may not be the best decision. When we realize our mistake, our pride compounds the problem with another misstep. Before we know it, we become entangled in a web of lies, cover-ups, and deception.

The story of David and Bathsheba is a classic biblical example. David was God's man, chosen to lead God's people. Bathsheba was the unlikely link between David and Solomon—Israel's two most famous kings. David witnessed God's sovereignty and experienced what it was to have God's hand protect him. Bathsheba's family served as counselor and bodyguard to the king.

David's pride and inappropriate choices led to big mistakes and catastrophic outcomes. Each decision contributed to a domino effect of very sad events. Yet God, in his mercy and grace, brought good from the ashes of sin. It was out of those ashes that Jesus, the Savior of humanity, was born to a descendant of David and Bathsheba.

Misdirected pride led David to cover up the sin of adultery with murder and lies that drove a wedge between God and himself and could have cost him his throne. But a merciful God sent Nathan to bring David to his senses and back to a right relationship with God.

David could have exacerbated the situation by denying what he had done and ordering Nathan executed for challenging the king. Instead, he admitted his sin and turned his heart back to God. After Nathan confronted David in 2 Samuel 12:1–15, he responded by pleading for mercy, forgiveness, and cleansing, as seen in Psalm 51.

David repented, and God forgave him. What a beautiful illustration of God's mercy and grace that is greater than all our sins. I am so grateful that God included this story in his Word. It's a reminder that when we allow ill-fated pride to take us down a road away from God, it won't end well. But when we swallow our pride and humbly call on God, no sin is too great to be forgiven.

Beware of Misleading Substitutions

God created some of us with a single exceptional ability and others with multiple talents. In each case, he expects us to dedicate those gifts to him for his glory. When we become discouraged or disappointed in what we believe God has called us to, those reactions can mislead us into using our talent or talents for something outside his plan. The grass appears greener and more welcoming on the other side, so we ask ourselves, "Why not use my talent over there?"

When I experienced what I saw as rejection by the church for what God called me to, I let misguided advice influence my decision to take my gifts and talents and use them in business. Mistake number one. When I continually decided to not make decisions based on God's Word, that was mistakes number two, three, four, and more.

Now, let me be clear; I'm not saying that God doesn't want you to provide leadership in the business, corporate, or political world. If he has called you there—wonderful. If God placed you there, he will guide you as you put your trust in him and seek his wisdom.

And there lies the key.

No matter where our leadership call takes us—ministry, business, politics, community, and so on—when we consistently seek him and rely on his wisdom, he blesses and uses us. But when we decide to take matters into our own hands and focus our talents and gifts in a direction he did not lay out for us, we will be miserable. Oh, we may have some success, but down deep, we'll know what's really going on. The wide-open, seeping wound won't heal. We'll go to bed at night, aware of the dark, gaping pit that grows deeper. We'll wake up in the morning, knowing another day needs to be faced alone. And we'll ask, "Where is God, anyway?"

And so it goes. We substitute a blessed life in God's will with whatever satisfies us at the time. Yes, there are happy moments along the way—accomplishments to be proud of, fun times to enjoy—but in the end, we sacrifice genuine joy.

Have you ever wondered what happened to Paul's friend, Demas? In Colossians 4:14, when Paul wrote from prison to the church at Colossae, he included greetings from Demas. In Philemon 24, he referred to Demas as "my fellow worker." But later, in 2 Timothy 4:10, Paul says, Demas "deserted me and has gone to Thessalonica."

Did Demas serve God in some other way, or did he abandon his faith all together and allow himself to be misled? It seems he started well and had a fruitful ministry, but Paul's last reference to him proclaims, "he deserted me." We're not told what happened, but somewhere along the way, things changed for Demas. Paul continues in 2 Timothy 2:10 by saying, Demas was "in love with this present world." In other words, it appears he turned his back on his friends and went to Thessalonica, the hub of trade where commerce was prominent and Christians were persecuted. Demas abandoned his ministry and allowed the substitutions of the world—wealth, power, pleasure—to mislead him.

As leaders, we must guard against misleading substitutions that could draw us away from God's perfect plan for our lives.

Beware of Mistaken Attitudes

God wants to use us, but the difference is in our heart's attitude. Are our motives pure? Or are we growing complacent to the needs of those around us? Do we have a heart of compassion, a humble, gentle, and quiet spirit, and a hunger and thirst for righteousness? Or are we losing the desire to care? Do we pursue peace while standing strong under pressure? Or are we secretly holding something against a fellow believer?

Matthew 5:23–24 tells us, "So if you are offering your gift at the altar and there remember that your brother has something against you, leave your gift there before the altar and go. First be reconciled to your brother, and then come and offer your gift."

There are two truths I see here.

First, it doesn't say, "if you have something against a brother." It says, "if your brother has something against you." Our natural response to hearing someone has something against us may be,

"That's their problem. They can come to me first." But that's not what Jesus was teaching here. Instead, we are to take the first step. Relationships with others must be in order if our gift is to be used to the fullest.

Second, it doesn't say, "take your gift with you and go your way." It says, "Leave your gift before the altar and go." If we come before God with our gifts and talents but need to reconcile a relationship, and desire to do so, then our heart attitude is right and God will not reject our gift. He merely asks that we "go" and make peace, then come back. With the right heart attitude, we are more available and prepared to be a God-honoring influence in a world full of negative influences.

Scripture gives separate accounts of two queens with influence. Queen Jezebel influenced her world negatively with her destructive and evil life, earning her God's wrath when he said, "The dogs shall eat Jezebel within the walls of Jezreel" (1 Kings 21:23).

Conversely, Queen Esther, as recorded in the book of Esther, influenced both the exiled Jews and the reigning Persians when God chose her to help preserve and build a nation for God.

God wants us as leaders to stand tall and together—not with a clenched fist of anger and hostility that leads to disunity and destruction, but with an open hand of servanthood and love that leads to growth and life. The choice is up to us.

Beware of Mismanaged Commitments

Some of us can juggle a lot at one time. We enjoy organizing our schedule to accomplish more in a day than seems humanly possible. We relish the idea of making multiple tasks come together within a deadline. Many label us as "high-capacity people." If you're nodding your head right now, then you're probably one of those people.

On the other hand, you may think the group I just described is strange. You get tired just thinking about everything you have to get done before the end of the week and prefer to take a coffee break first. If that's you, then you're probably like my husband, who says, "I do one thing at a time. I do it very well. Then I move on."

Both groups of people have commitments to be managed, but they manage them differently. One group is no better than the other—just different. And that's okay. God created us to be unique. But he also expects us to manage the commitments he's given us in a way that honors him.

In Exodus 18:13–27, we see Moses's father-in-law, Jethro, confronting Moses about his heavy workload and commitments. During the forty years Moses spent living with or near Jethro after he fled from Egypt, Jethro had a front-row seat to watch God shape the rising leader. Based on how Moses greeted Jethro in the desert (Exodus 18:7), shared all God had done for the Israelites (Exodus 18:8), and quickly took Jethro's advice (Exodus 18:24), it seems they had a close relationship. There was a give and take in their friendship and a mutual desire to serve God. Jethro was not an Israelite but became a worshipper of the true God.

It's possible Moses thought he had to serve as judge over the people, but in fact, there were others equally capable of helping carry the load. He was so busy listening to disputes from morning until evening that he didn't have time to step back as a leader and look at the big picture. It took the practicality of Jethro and his ability to troubleshoot and organize to show Moses there was a better way.

Whether we're high-capacity individuals or one-thing-at-a-time people, we can fall into the trap of mismanaging our commitments. One commitment can pull us in the wrong direction, and many commitments can cause us to head in no direction. Whether we're juggling one commitment or ten, we can feel so overwhelmed that we want to quit everything.

God never intended us to get under the load so that we complain or want to give up. We can commit ourselves to many good things, but when they're not the right things according to God's plan or they're done with the wrong motives, they are nothing.

One day, a man from the Missionaries of Charity, founded by Mother Teresa to serve "the poorest of the poor," came to her complaining about a superior whose rules, he felt, were interfering with his ministry. He was being assigned responsibilities that took him away from his work with the lepers.

"My vocation is to work for lepers," he said. "I want to spend myself for the lepers."

After staring at him for a moment, Mother Teresa smiled and gently replied, "Brother, your vocation is not to work for lepers; your vocation is to belong to Jesus."[8]

If we desire to serve God where he called us to lead, our priority is our relationship with him. The other tasks and responsibilities we commit ourselves to will then happen out of love and commitment to our Savior.

Misdirected pride, misleading substitutions, mistaken attitudes, and mismanaged commitments are only four potential traps that can draw us into a desolate wilderness. And believe me, it can happen to anyone. But know this: God chose you, God wants you, and God knows your name. Your weakness, your brokenness, or your sin does not shock him. He loves you and holds you in his almighty hand.

Part 3

RESCUED BY GRACE

The faithfulness of God wraps us in his enduring love
and amazing grace.

The Road Back

God puts us in a tight place to bring us to the right place.
—Ann Griffiths

By now, you may think you're reading a memoir rather than a book about leadership. But isn't leadership part of life? Isn't life part of leadership?

Work. Ministry. Personal. Each aspect of our lives intertwines with the others to create a map full of valleys, mountains, roadways, and yes, sometimes a desert or two. That's life. Along the way, the valleys offer a peaceful place to rest awhile or plunge us into deep regret. Mountain experiences give us a sense of victorious accomplishment or throw us off balance as we teeter on the edge of a precarious ledge. Highways and pathways amaze us at every turn or trip us up when we're surprised by a detour or a bump in the road.

We've almost come to expect the extremes of life's valleys, mountains, and roadways. But when we find ourselves in a desert or wilderness place, our very life can feel threatened. We struggle to hold it all together while life continues around us.

Think of yourself on a journey that takes you into a desert. You have a map with milestones plainly marked. You have a clear vision of where you're going. Each landmark is a goal to be reached along the way. You're following what you believe will get you from point A to point B. But it's not the ride you expected.

It reminds me of my friend Bobbie, and her story about the time she ventured into a vast desert.

⁓

Bobbie flung her hand around to the side pouch of her pack, pulled out a tattered map, unfolded it, and scanned for a safe place to hide.

"In minutes, it'll be too late," she whispered to herself as she pressed her finger on the wrinkled map and glanced up at the horizon. "I must find shelter. Now.

"Here's something. Lone Rock. It's just over that hill." Quickly, she jammed the paper back into its pouch, shifted the load on her back, and ran for safety.

Though Bobbie was an experienced trekker and loved adventure, she had checked in with a merchant at the market before leaving the village at the edge of the desert. But his words were a little too ominous for her liking.

"When sandstorms hit, they come hard and fast. The sand shifts, and the landscape changes. Maps are no help at all. And without a compass, you won't find your way back."

"I'll be fine," she'd assured him, before heading out. "The sky is clear, and I'll be gone for only a few hours. But I promise to take my compass."

Earlier, she'd read that the sands could appear calm and peaceful yet become violent and ruthless in a short time. Gentle sand could swirl up from the ground and, under the command of sudden merciless winds, transform soft rolling dunes into a blinding, relentless storm that renders maps obsolete.

This map has to be right. Lone Rock has to be there. If it isn't, I'm doomed, she thought as she ran for cover.

While she was midstride, something hit her leg and bounced to the ground.

Stop. A silent voice demanded. *You must go back and pick it up.*

Glancing over her shoulder at the horizon, Bobbie's pace slowed. The threatening mass was gaining momentum as the persistent voice pounded. *Go back. Pick it up.*

"There's no time." She argued to herself. "I don't even know what hit my leg." Impulsively, she turned and dashed back a few yards. There in the sand lay her partially buried compass with its face to the sky. After scooping it up, she turned and retraced her steps up the dune that stood between her and safety. From its crest, the only solid thing visible for miles was Lone Rock.

With one final glance back toward the menacing cloud of sand closing in on her, Bobbie scrambled down the desert slope to a collection of large boulders with openings big enough for one person. Pulling her pack off, she dropped to her knees and dove into the hole that faced away from the imminent sandstorm.

Wedging her pack against the opening, she buried her chin into her chest, pulled her shirt up to hide her face, and curled into a ball to protect herself from the angry wind and sand that forced themselves against the walls of her sanctuary. The howling darkness cradled her exhausted body, and she slept.

By the time Bobbie woke up, silence had overtaken the sounds of fury. Light peeked through cracks between the rocks and reflected off a metal clip on her backpack, which the outside build-up of sand had pushed further into the cave.

"Oh, my eyes," she moaned as her eyelids scraped against themselves. "And my lungs; they feel like half the desert's on my chest."

Slowly, she took deep breaths as she peered through the small opening at a distorted landscape of alien shapes. She forced her stiff body through the opening, then stood upright outside the cave and shook the sand from her hair and clothes. Dust had replaced clean air, and she struggled to breathe as she reached for her map. She had to find her way back to the village.

Deliberately, she turned the map toward every direction and looked out over the sand. "It doesn't matter which way I look. Nothing out there matches the marks on the map," she mumbled as she recalled the village merchant's warning:

"When sandstorms hit, maps are useless. You need a compass."

Frustrated, she crushed the map in her hand and stuffed it into her pocket. As she pulled her hand out, something fell to the ground and landed face up on the sand beside her.

Storms may be prevalent in your life. An unexpected catastrophe turned your life upside down, and you feel your faith crumbling. Your reputation is being threatened. Overwhelming doubt and fear are overtaking you like an anchor around your neck, and you long to experience the thrill you first felt when you started your journey. It's a merciless desert place where hope is buried deep in the whirling sands of the storm. You know if you don't do something soon, you may not survive.

My road back to ministry and a renewed reality of God in my life was not an easy one. By the time my wilderness journey came to an explosive climax in January 1992, I'd been stumbling around for about four years. Yet, I was soon to learn my wanderings were not yet over.

It's hard to explain what the next twelve years were like. In some ways, they crept by. In other ways, life was a whirlwind of events, activities, and changes. On the surface, it looked like I was successful. Yet, all along, I struggled to find my way.

My business continued to see normal ups and downs until, in 1994, I received a call from a client offering me what many would see as a dream job.

I had pursued this client for two years before they hired my agency to help them with their marketing and advertising needs. Now, they wanted to hire me personally to head up their marketing department. Wow—what an opportunity. I would work at their corporate head office and interact with franchisees across the country. However, I'd also be starting from scratch with no staff in the department. In other words, I would be the marketing department—at least in the beginning.

I've always loved developing things from the ground up, so the offer appealed to me. But before I gave my answer, I weighed the pros and cons. When I finally made my decision and ventured into an industry that outside observers often viewed as glamorous, my staff and contract team did not want me to close my company. Instead, they proposed to stay on and maintain the business, believing I could oversee everything from a distance. To me, that wasn't a viable option. I knew when I took something on, I was an all-or-nothing, full-speed-ahead kind of person. Trying to divide my attention between two businesses would only dilute my effectiveness.

I took the plunge, wound down my agency, and geared up for employment in someone else's business. I knew one person couldn't do all the needed strategic planning, budgeting, media buying, creative design, copywriting, promotions, and more. However, over the years, I had developed working relationships with entrepreneurs whose businesses focused on each of those areas, and they had become my friends.

To help meet the demands of my new role, I approached those friends, one at a time. The result was a powerhouse of businesswomen who each brought their expertise to the table. Collectively, they formed my outside marketing and advertising resource team while maintaining their own independent companies. And what a team they were.

Each woman had her own personality and style, but they respected one another's skills and worked seamlessly together. Eventually, I hired in-house staff and grew the department while continuing to use the specialized skills of my outside team. Interestingly, the staff I hired were university marketing graduates with youthful eagerness, teachable ambition, and nothing-is-impossible attitudes that complemented the seasoned experience of those on my resource team.

It was a fast-paced life of travel, meetings, late nights, and deadlines. Sometimes, I raced to the airport, flew into a different time zone, checked into a hotel, schmoozed with suppliers or clients, tried to grab some sleep, then sat in meetings before flying home the next day. On some occasions, I took a suitcase to work, walked or took a cab to the harbor that I could see from my office window, boarded a ship with some of my peers for a two- or three-night marathon of business socializing and meetings, then disembarked back where we started and headed straight to the office for a full day's work before heading home.

Over the next five years as I was driven to meet high-level corporate demands, Jim and I worked to rebuild our marriage. Yet, while God and I were still not on close speaking terms, I somehow maintained a sense of knowing he existed.

The closest I got to a church was in 1995 when we celebrated the marriage of our daughter, Sarah, and her amazing Sherman. With three months to plan, friends came alongside to help organize a beautiful wedding with two hundred guests in attendance. My next forays into church were when Sarah and Sherman had their two children in 1997 and 1998, and we attended their dedications in the church they were attending.

In 1999, after working as vice president of marketing for this fast-growing, marketing-driven company and seeing it grow from seventeen offices to 150 across North America, I said goodbye to the corporate world and believed that, at forty-eight years of age, I might like to retire early.

I spent the next few days in isolation, reading and quietly contemplating *what now?* Systematically, I went through exercises to identify my core values and think about my goals. The experience was an eye-opener. I came to realize I struggled most when my involvements conflicted with who I really was at my core. I also believe that, though I didn't realize it, those few days of reflection shed light on the first marker God set down to help me find my way out of the wilderness. But my wanderings were still not yet over.

When word got out that I was no longer employed, I began receiving requests to do contract work on the side. Was this another business opportunity? I didn't know. But I knew I wasn't one to sit still for very long. And I could use the money.

One client I engaged sent my husband and me to London, England, to conduct business expansion research. It was a wonderful combination of work, relaxation, and visiting relatives. It also gave Jim and me the time to focus on us. The boutique hotel we stayed in was a quaint, old-English building with rich woods and custom furnishings, reminiscent of days gone by.

One evening as we sat in upholstered wingback chairs by the stone fireplace in the lounge area, we talked about our life together. We shared some of our sad moments and laughed at the daring escapades we'd experienced. We recounted adventures we'd undertaken and survived. And we reflected on people who had fed into our lives and those who were no longer with us. Our reminiscing was a pivotal point in our rebuilding process.

A few days after our return, I received a call from the graphic designer who had been my first hire when I initially embarked on my journey into the business world.

"Ann, what are you doing on Monday?" she asked after we exchanged niceties that Saturday afternoon. "I could really use your help."

"For you, I'll clear whatever's on my calendar. What do you need?"

As she talked, I learned that in two days her growing advertising agency was making a presentation to the largest potential client she had ever entertained, and they were up against some stiff competition. Winning this account would make a world of difference for their future. But she'd had an emergency on her team and was short on a specific staff role.

The next day, Sunday, I spent hours being briefed at my friend's offices so I could effectively take part in the presentation the next day. Signing the nondisclosure documents, getting up to speed on company procedures and operations, and learning all I could about the potential client was intense, but vital.

Thanks to a talented and well-prepared team, we won the account. Before the end of the week, they asked me to join the agency and oversee their client services. As Jim and I were now empty nesters and both needing to commute to work, we rented out our home in the suburbs and leased a condo one block from my office in downtown Vancouver.

Within the year, my friend offered me a partnership and together we embarked on the roller coaster ride that's often felt by partners of growing companies. When she moved to another country, I continued to run our operations from the Canadian office while she worked remotely. Together, we maintained a comfortable staff-client ratio. And we grew.

Then on September 11, 2001, we woke up to the tragic events of what is now known as 9/11.

Sadly, our business was drastically affected, and after struggling for another year and a half, my partner and I made the torturous decision to close our company. Sitting in my living room surrounded by the remaining mountains of files and boxes we had moved to my home for sorting, I asked myself, "Now what do I do when I grow up?"

As I pored over the details involved in closing a company, I again reflected on my life. I revisited the values I had identified years earlier, made a list of all the things I enjoyed doing, and narrowed that list down to the activities I could make a living at. Next, I turned to my computer, plugged keywords into search engines, explored possibilities that fit within my criteria, and discovered professional coaching. I'd never heard of this relatively new industry but was definitely curious. Little did I know God was placing a major marker in my way that would lead me back to him.

We may start out being strong, outspoken, and vigilant in serving God. But when we realize we've wandered into a desert place, we wonder what on earth got us there. None of us is invincible. None of us is immune. Satan's goal is to crush and destroy God's chosen ones. He will use countless pitfalls to keep us from going back and picking up the compass we once carried. He'll set traps to hinder us from finding our way home, like with my friend Bobbie in the desert.

Simon Peter was a bold and ardent follower of Jesus. Yet in Luke 22:31–34, Jesus warned Peter that he would deny him. When I read the account of that warning, I was struck by the deep love Jesus expressed to Peter when he told him Satan demanded to have him. "But I have pleaded in prayer for you, Simon, that your faith should not fail" (Luke 22:32 NLT).

Jesus then followed those words with a powerful statement about the work God had for Peter. "So when you have repented and turned to me again, strengthen your brothers" (Luke 22:32 NLT). Jesus knew Peter would deny him. But Jesus also knew Peter would repent. Jesus assured Peter that although his faith would falter, it would not be destroyed. Instead, it would be renewed, and he'd become the leader God chose him to be.

Peter's experience gives us hope and confidence that Jesus loves us, pleads for us, and will use us again when we repent. Maybe you struggle with that truth. I know I did. How could God possibly forgive and restore me to his service when I'd wasted fifteen years doing everything but acknowledging and serving him?

My journey took me to a place where I questioned the very existence of God. Yet through it all, he held me in the hollow of his hand. Jesus pleaded for me and set markers for me to see. All I needed to do was pick up my compass and open my eyes.

Like Peter, maybe you served God faithfully and passionately, but now you're in a wilderness or right on the edge of one. My friend, take it from one who's been there—Jesus is pleading for you right now.

Chapter 10

Easy Does It

When I could not come to where he was, he came to me.
—Squire Parsons

While finalizing the closing of our business and dealing with the pressures that came with it, I was determined to finish the university graduate work I had begun a couple of years earlier. Within the year, it was mission accomplished. But, not knowing what the future held, I continued to pore over websites and information about this new vocation known as coaching. Transition and change were in the air. Was I catching a glimpse of what could be a major pivot point in my life?

During this time, I also enjoyed the slower pace of being at home—not bombarded by phone calls, emails, deadlines or a tight schedule. I soaked in the view from our downtown condo, reflected, journaled, and spent time with our grandbabies. I also read books and wondered if I could ever get back to writing.

Years before, I had taken creative writing courses and joined a writers' group with my daughter. It had been difficult to maintain personal writing activities while entrenched in the demands of work and school. As I circled this rising pivot point in my life, I explored writing again and rejoined the writers' group, who welcomed me back with open arms. I didn't work on any specific writing projects but found it was a healthy way to release pent-up thoughts. When Jim and I decided it was an activity we could do together, he also became part of the group. And I discovered again how much I enjoyed writing.

Meanwhile in my continued research about coaching, I connected with someone whose name kept popping up on different websites. I later learned he had earned the designation of "master coach," was highly respected in the industry, and was successful in his business. He was also more than willing to answer my questions and point me in helpful directions.

When he suggested I attend an introductory workshop being offered in my city by a reputable California school, I signed up.

Confidently, he said, "Ann, by the end of the weekend, you will know whether coaching is a direction for you to pursue." He was right.

A circle of individuals from various backgrounds welcomed me in. Though different from one another, we had common interests and a desire to grow. These were nice people. However, as I listened to the teaching, I sensed it didn't all line up with the biblical teachings that somehow clung tenaciously to my inner being. I knew I was supposed to be there because everything was connecting deep within me. Yet it surprised me how much past biblical awareness pushed its way to the surface to act as a measuring stick. All kinds of philosophies and life perspectives had entered my world, from New Age to Buddhism to flat-out unbelief in anything. But God was making his voice heard. I now know he was being true to his word and bringing light out of darkness (Psalm 18:28).

Following the first weekend, I signed up for four more full weekends of study. By the end of the summer of 2003, I applied to the school and began my journey toward becoming a certified professional coach.

When my studies and exams were finally complete, I felt armed with education credentials, business experience, and enthusiasm. I had a website and business cards designed, created online communications, and developed workshop outlines and materials. I also networked and gave complimentary, sample coaching sessions to prospective clients. Most people in my class took the training to focus on life coaching, but I concentrated on coaching business owners and their teams. As clients came onboard, they benefited from the coaching, and my business thrived. In time, my clients also included ministry leaders and their teams.

I didn't see it then, but I now realize God continually protected me and placed markers in my path to help me find my way out of the wilderness. On numerous occasions, especially during my coach training, I encountered people and teachings that sounded wonderful, almost scriptural. But then a Bible verse I had learned or spoken about in the past popped into my mind to reveal the truth. It was as if God was raising flags of warning—evidence of his ongoing protection, even when I wasn't actively seeking it.

When my coaching venture was barely off the ground, our daughter and son-in-law approached us with a question we weren't expecting at the time. "Mom? Dad? Are you ready to move out of the city and into a place together?"

We'd always talked about sharing a home, but was this the time? Sarah and Sherman were definitely ready. Their children were starting school, Sherman was trying to start a business, and they'd outgrown their matchbox basement suite.

Jim and I reasoned that there was no longer anything to keep us in the city, and I could do my coaching business from anywhere. If I needed to meet face-to-face with clients, I could drive to them. In no time, we were ready to move.

Within two weeks of our mutual agreement, Sarah found a house farther away from the city than I imagined we would go. But once we all inspected it, there was consensus—it met our needs. Within two months, on April 24, 2004, we all moved into our new home, about forty-five miles from Vancouver.

On the first morning Jim and I woke up in our new-to-us home, I remember saying, "Do you hear that?"

"What? I don't hear a thing."

"Exactly," I chuckled. "It's so quiet."

After living in the busy downtown core of the city, close to the hustle and bustle of work and never-ending street noise, we soaked in the silence. We'd moved into a small neighborhood, and all we could hear was a dog barking in the distance.

In one year, my career transitioned from the familiar marketing and advertising arena to the previously unknown-to-me business of coaching. My studies were complete, although the learning would continue. Our living situation drastically changed, and our marriage gained strength. The pivot point was genuine. But it was only the beginning.

I was grateful I could conduct coaching sessions over the phone or on face-to-face conference calls. But I also enjoyed the weekly drive to meet with clients in the city. During those long, highway drive times, I reflected and planned. It was my time. It was also the place and time God interrupted my thinking, as if to say, *Okay, Ann, it's now my turn.*

As I drove, I thought about the previous years. When Grandma passed, I experienced a plague of unsettling years and ran from God. Yet, on those quiet drives, he soothed my mind with music that rushed from the vault of my memory. I spontaneously sang songs like "Jesus Loves Me" or "The Love of God" or "Marvelous Grace." The words drilled deep into my thoughts as my heart grasped their deeper meaning and richness.

It had been about fifteen years since we were involved in a church. During our last year or so of living in the downtown core of Vancouver, Jim periodically convinced me to go to church with him, hoping to find somewhere to call home. But while I still struggled, God remained patient, and Jim gave me space to think about whatever I needed to work through.

The closest we came to finding a church in the city was when we walked to one built well over a hundred years ago. It was a stately building with stained-glass windows and rising arches. The solid-but-creaky wooden benches welcomed us in their own strange way. For me, the music was the most wonderful part of the morning. When the service ended and someone sat at the massive pipe organ to play Bach, it riveted me. Rich tones flooded the height and width of the room. My eyes filled with tears, and the soul of the music overflowed into my spirit like it was a dry sponge left outside in a spring rain. Sadly, we returned to the church only once, but that first experience ignited a faint spark within me.

On one of my summer drives home from meeting with a client, I inadvertently took a different exit off the highway. The route took me right by a church I'd never attended but was familiar with because it was part of the same denomination I'd served in years before. In the morning, I asked Jim if he'd like to check it out. Though surprised, he agreed.

The next Sunday, Jim and I drove into the already full parking lot. Would the church be a good fit for where we were on our journey?

Before getting out of the car, Jim turned and asked, "Are you ready for this?"

"No, I'm not ready. So don't leave me alone." I wanted to sit quietly near the back, melt into the crowd, and not have anyone recognize me. I certainly didn't want to have to answer questions like, "Where have you been all these years?"

What I didn't know was that this church had a reputation for its friendliness. As soon as we walked through the front doors, people greeted us warmly. We were five cities away from where we spent most of our previous years, yet here were people we knew.

It wasn't long before I realized my attempt to be invisible was only secure as long as I didn't smile or say anything. I guess we can change our appearances, but there are some things, like our smile and voice, that are hard to mask.

After the service, people mingled in the lobby. There was no mistake; people knew us, and we knew them. Some were individuals from our childhood and teenage years—people who had powerfully influenced us. There was now-retired Pastor Handy, who was my pastor when I was a little girl and who had mentored Jim when we first met. There was Pastor Lawrence, who'd married us years before in a different church and who was now a member of this congregation with his wife. The president of Trinity Western University was also there with his wife, as well as Dave, my former boss from the same school, with his wife—and more.

So many familiar folks from years gone by stepped up to welcome us. They talked about when we'd served together in ministry or recounted a time when they had heard me speak. But they didn't know the "me" of the past fifteen years. I felt awkward—like a stranger among friends. Yet on that Sunday, the people and memories exposed a longing for connection I didn't realize was missing.

When we got into our car to leave, my first words to Jim were, "I feel like I'm home."

Over the summer and into the fall of 2004, we attended the church sporadically. As the year drew to a close, we put our roots down and became regular attenders. But I was still on my guard.

Sitting in church, I hoped no one saw me fumble through my Bible to find the passages being read from the platform. I remembered where to find Genesis, Psalms, the Gospels, and Revelation. But everything in between was like being in an old-fashioned Bible drill with one hand behind my back and my brain on hold. My confidence collided with my pride, and I felt like a novice. The pages of my once-treasured Bible stuck together from lack of use. I wrestled with the secrets hidden deep inside me. How could God love me? Did he really want me back? Would this church accept me if they knew where I'd been or what I'd done? I wasn't sure. But I knew I needed to reacquaint myself with God and my Bible.

Matthew 27:1–5 recounts when Judas betrayed Jesus and turned him over to the authorities. When he "realized that Jesus had been condemned to die, he was filled with remorse" (Matthew 27:3 NLT).

To right his wrong, Judas tried to return the money to the priests and elders, saying, "I have sinned, for I have betrayed an innocent man."

But their response was, "What do we care? That's your problem."

Judas then threw the money down, went out, and hung himself.

Though Judas didn't seem to have a problem betraying Jesus, it was a step too far when he learned the authorities had judged, sentenced, and scheduled Jesus to die. He seemed willing to betray someone he had committed himself to but did not want to be implicated in his murder. When he realized the severity of what he'd done, he couldn't live with himself.

Like Judas, Peter also betrayed Jesus—three times, no less. When he denied him the third time, he refused to acknowledge knowing Jesus, and basically said, "May God strike me dead if I'm lying." When the rooster crowed and Peter remembered Jesus's warning that "Before the rooster crows today, you will deny me three times," he understood what he had done and "wept bitterly" (Luke 22:61). But, unlike Judas, Peter acknowledged his sin of betrayal, confessed it, and accepted forgiveness, allowing God to mold him into the man who would build and lead the fledgling church.

Two men lived as friends for three years. Two men betrayed Jesus. When they grasped what they had done, both men were remorseful. Two men with front-row seats to seeing Jesus heal, comfort, provide, and forgive others. Yet, when each man stumbled and failed, their responses and outcomes were totally different.

Peter faced his guilt head-on. Judas saw his guilt as a mountain he couldn't climb. Peter believed that what Jesus did for others also applied to him. Judas couldn't accept those same things for himself. Peter's response was to confess his sin, accept forgiveness, and commit himself in a deeper way. Judas's response was to commit suicide. He couldn't see himself the way Jesus saw him.

Isn't that like so many of us? We see ourselves for what we did or didn't do. We see our mixed-up emotions, our doubts, our shortcomings, our sin. And as we focus on those things, the guilt increases. Sadly, like Judas, the guilt becomes overwhelming, and we get stuck in misery.

Effective leaders and people who are strong in their faith can stumble, fall, and get stuck in a pit of despair. Sometimes, they simply can't get past the guilt that entrenched itself deep within them. Eventually, they walk away from God and the church or sit disengaged on the back pew.

I came to realize that if I was ever going to serve again and fulfill God's plan for me, I had to start with baby steps—accepting God's view of me, accepting his love and forgiveness, and trusting that he knew the way out of my wilderness and beyond.

Chapter 11

Learning to Walk Again

*It is always hard to see the purpose in wilderness
wanderings until after they are over.*
—John Bunyan

In January 2017, I broke my right ankle in three places and tore the main ligament running the top length of my foot. It was not a fun time—at all. My busy schedule came to an abrupt halt. It forced me to be immobile and let others take care of me. Pain was an ever-present companion. Each day, I tried whatever I could to speed up the recovery but quickly learned that trying to rush the process was not the smartest thing I'd ever done. Even my big toe didn't cooperate. If I could just start small and get it to wiggle a little, I'd feel like I was getting somewhere. But whenever I tried the slightest movement, it just sat there—peeking over the edge of my cast and mocking me from its safe vantage point.

As weeks passed, my activity levels increased. I graduated from casts to bandages and from hobbling on crutches to walking with a cane, then a limp—until my gait was normal. It seemed to take a long time to rebuild my strength and confidence. But as movement improved, I could take on the activities that previously brought so much joy. By letting go of pride, learning to be still, and clinging tenaciously to the knowledge that God was in control of even this, life gradually got back to normal.

During my recovery, I reflected on what had transpired during the first year and a half following our move from the city. Had God laid me up to remind me of the journey I took when I learned to walk with him again?

Though we were sporadic in our church attendance through-out the fall of 2004, the lead pastor and his wife invited us to join a small group that met in their home every Sunday night. It was a start. By the end of December, we were regular church attendees. It was about that time I stepped out and introduced myself to the church worship director. Crystal Hicks was, and still is, a gifted worship leader and award-winning, international recording artist who oozes warmth and joy. Her genuine commitment to serve God and her sensitivity to people makes anyone and everyone feel significant and comfortable around her. She loves people and they love her.

Crystal and I had known each other years before. While she continued on as a popular vocalist, I had sacrificed many bonds with fellow musicians, and my love for playing music became a casualty of my wilderness journey.

Following a Sunday service, I walked toward the front of the church where Crystal was engaged in conversation with other peo-ple. I was pretty sure she didn't know I'd been warming a spot on one of the back pews for the past few weeks, trying to regain my church bearings. Would she even remember me? About fifteen years had passed, and I'd already been told by others in the church that they didn't recognize me.

Hesitantly, I stepped forward. "Hi, Crystal."

Focusing her broad smile and welcoming eyes toward me, she replied, "Hi."

"You don't remember me, do you?"

"I'm not sure."

"Ann. Ann Griffiths."

As her mind seemed to reach back in time to light a spark of memory, recognition swept over her face. We spent a few minutes exchanging niceties before she had to redirect her attention to other people waiting to talk with her. That moment launched a mutual friendship that deepened and continues to this day.

Shortly after Christmas, Crystal asked if I'd be interested in playing drums with a worship team she was putting together for an upcoming women's conference.

"Oh, Crystal, I don't know." I balked. "Over the past fifteen years, I haven't even picked up a pair of drumsticks, let alone play."

She smiled gently and shot back, "Ann, once ya got it, ya got it. I'm sure you'll be just fine. Rehearsals begin in a month, so let me know as soon as you can."

Crystal's timing couldn't have been better. During the previous couple of months, I had wondered what it would be like to play again. Would God have a place for me? Was Crystal's invitation a nod and smile from God in that direction?

When weekly rehearsals began, I didn't know any of the other seven women except Crystal. I also quickly realized how much music had changed since my church involvement years before. I was a fish out of water, flapping around in unknown territory. Yet though the music was all new to me, playing was like riding a bike—you never really forget. It felt natural and energizing, and I loved the challenge.

Leading up to the two-day conference in early March 2005, I became more and more nervous. For the first time in fifteen years,

I was about to attend a women's event and play drums in public. It was a double whammy. When my daughter, Sarah, agreed to attend the conference with me, I felt like a child going to her first recital with her mother sitting in the audience to cheer her on. I can't tell you how wonderful it was to look into a sea of roughly two hundred women and see Sarah's smiling and encouraging face.

Besides the joy of playing drums on a worship team again, two things stood out to me at that conference. The first was when I strolled out to the lobby where tables displayed books for sale. God was renewing my interest in ministry—even though the thought was just between him and me. I wanted to see what was now being written and read by Christian women. To my surprise, the topics and writings were similar to fifteen years prior when I was an avid reader of anything on women and leadership and other topics of interest. The only thing that seemed to have changed was the artwork on the book covers.

I remember feeling disappointed, almost frustrated. Were we still struggling with the same concerns? Had we not moved beyond gender issues in the church or the things that tried to hold us back from being all God intended us to be? Had nothing changed?

Second, I remember a panel discussion hosted by a popular producer and moderator of a Christian TV program. I don't recall what the panel's primary focus was, but I remember what one woman said in response to a question directed at her. In her answer, she referred to a difficult period in her life and called it a wilderness.

My ears perked up, and I wrote in my notes, "Wilderness." That was it. Since returning to church and getting back into the right relationship with God, I struggled with feeling like I had wasted fifteen years. I wondered what on earth I'd been doing and where I was headed. And there it was—wilderness. It couldn't be plainer. I'd been wandering around, lost in a wilderness.

When the host asked the panelist, "When did you come out of the wilderness and how long were you in it?" her answer inspired me with hope.

"It was about twelve years," she replied. "But I don't really know when I came to the end of the wilderness or that I've even come to the end."

I too wasn't sure I was out of my wilderness. But I knew I was on the right track.

Through the next year, I continued building my coaching business, took on some business and ministry speaking engagements, played drums on the church worship team with Crystal, and spent time with friends and family. I also began reading current books on women and leadership and what was happening in churches and ministries for women. That one word, *wilderness*, put my mind at peace. I may not yet have been completely out of that great desert, but I sensed I was on my way and on the edge of an adventure God was about to unfold for me—in his time.

When I received an invitation to be the keynote speaker at the church's women's retreat, I was nervous, yet excited. It was to be the first time in fifteen years that I'd spoken to a retreat full of Christian women. I felt ill-equipped but accepted the invitation as a nod from God and whispered, "Okay, Lord, here I am."

Again, Sarah came with me. This time, she took part. At the beginning of each session, she performed a short pantomime to set the scene for the topic. It worked beautifully.

As I reflect on the theme of that March 2006 weekend, I'm reminded that when we resist stepping out or away from what holds us back, we short-circuit God's perfect will for us. When we step up and acknowledge that we sabotaged our relationship with God by the choices we made, there is reconciliation and restoration. Finally, when we step into God's perfect work and life for us, it takes courage, but we do not do it in our own strength or for our own glory. Rather, it is God who works in us, both to will and to work for his good pleasure (Philippians 2:13).

I was learning it wasn't about me. It was God who raised me up out of the dark pit I'd dug for myself with unwise decisions and obstinate pride. It was he who rescued me by his grace and gave the assurance that he would carry me through every opportunity he brought my way. I simply had to step forward and place my hand in his.

No matter how tarnished or ugly we may feel or how insignificant we think we are, God has a purpose for each of us. As leaders, we need to accept that truth for ourselves and for those we lead.

There are many biblical characters who learned to walk again. Some lived in palaces, others in humble homes, but they all had their spheres of influence. They were women and men who simply lived their lives—until something turned their worlds upside down and backward. For some, the change came because of choices they made. For others, it happened through circumstances beyond their control.

Take Naomi, for example. She was a woman who followed her husband when he uprooted his family to head for greener pastures on the other side of the Dead Sea. A famine was raging in their homeland of Judah, but it looked like the foreign land of Moab held promise. Following the arduous move, everything seemed to go well for Naomi and her family—until her husband, Elimelech, died and left Naomi widowed with two sons. In time, the two sons married Moabite women, and again, all seemed to go well until Naomi's two sons also died, leaving her and her two daughters-in-law widows.

Being a widow in the ancient world was almost worse than death. Society often ignored or took advantage of them, and they usually lived in poverty. In that period of history, God's law stipulated that the nearest relative of the dead husband was to care for

126

the widow. But Naomi had no relatives in Moab and didn't even know if she had relatives still alive in her homeland.

Knowing she faced an uncertain future, Naomi encouraged her daughters-in-law to start their lives over in Moab while she returned to Bethlehem, Judah. Orpah agreed to stay, but Ruth insisted on following Naomi. It appears Naomi's faith had such an impact on Ruth that she made the choice to leave her home and family to go with Naomi to her land and people. When she realized Ruth would not go back, Naomi conceded, and the two went on to Bethlehem together.

"Ruth said, 'Do not urge me to leave you or to return from following you. For where you go I will go, and where you lodge, I will lodge. Your people shall be my people, and your God my God'" (Ruth 1:16).

Naomi's influence contributed to Ruth making a life-changing decision. But, at this crucial uncertain time, we see a change in Naomi. Somewhere in her life journey, Naomi's faith wavered, and she became bitter. On her return to Bethlehem, she announced she no longer wanted to be called Naomi, meaning pleasant, but Mara, meaning bitter.

"She said to them, 'Do not call me Naomi; call me Mara, for the Almighty has dealt very bitterly with me'" (Ruth 1:20).

By changing her name, Naomi acknowledged that her heart had grown bitter. She blamed God for the grief, disappointments, and tragedies that permeated her life. Yet down deep and by God's grace, Naomi's faith in God somehow survived.

When Boaz, a relative, showed kindness to Ruth as she gleaned in his fields, Naomi praised God for it. She was bitter toward God, but it's clear she still believed in his goodness. When she heard the news about Boaz, God ignited a flicker of hope. Maybe there was a future for them, after all.

The story of Naomi, Ruth, and Boaz is all about redemption.

Naomi loved Ruth deeply and wanted the best for her. When she heard about Boaz, her first thought was of Ruth's well-being. She instructed Ruth to do what may seem strange to us but was consistent with Jewish custom and law. Ruth's obedience, her trust in Naomi, and her love for her prepared the way for God's purposes to be fulfilled in and through them, and ultimately affected future generations. Ruth was to become the great-grandmother of King David and named in the lineage of Jesus, whose life and sacrifice made it possible for generations upon generations to experience God's redemptive power and faithfulness.

The book of Ruth primarily focuses on Ruth and her kinsman-redeemer, Boaz, and foretells the coming of Jesus Christ, our Redeemer. Yet, Naomi's part in the story shows us that even though we may go through tough times and wander into a wilderness, God is faithful. Naomi may have lingered on the edge of a wilderness of despair and bitterness, but her faith in God did not completely die. God provided a kinsman-redeemer through Boaz that turned Ruth and Naomi's world around.

Like them, we don't know the greater purposes God is fulfilling through us, but his faithfulness to us is sure, for all generations. We are just one in a long line of generations, but he knows the part we play in his bigger plan. And he will not leave us.

Just as Naomi returned to Bethlehem where, generations later, Jesus the Messiah would be born, so he returns us to where he wants us if we allow him to fulfill his plan in us.

It's interesting that the only time we see Naomi referred to as Mara is when she herself told the people to call her that name when she returned to Bethlehem. God was already at work in her and guiding her back to where he needed her to be, but she didn't yet see it. She only saw the tragedy and bitterness that grew in her. Yet, those who were around her and watched the story unfold, saw God's provision for her.

"Then the women said to Naomi, 'Blessed be the LORD, who has not left you this day without a redeemer, and may his name be renowned in Israel! He shall be to you a restorer of life and a nourisher of your old age, for your daughter-in-law who loves you, who is more to you than seven sons, has given birth to him'" (Ruth 4:14–15).

In the closing verses of the final chapter of the book of Ruth, after the birth of Ruth and Boaz's son, we get a taste of God's love for Naomi by how he blesses her for her obedience. As the lights go down on this redemptive love story, we're treated to an encore—a tender moment in verse sixteen where we read, "Then Naomi took the child in her arms and cared for him" (Ruth 4:16 NIV).

Despite Naomi's broken life, she could learn to walk again and fulfill her part in God's grand plan. She did not know what future lay ahead for her little grandson. Only God knew he would grow up to become the grandfather of King David, whom God called, "A man after my own heart."

How often do we, like Naomi, focus our eyes on problems and disappointments, when all along God wants to bring us to the place where we'll fulfill his greater purpose? What are you focusing on? A problem? A disappointment? Successes? Failures? Or God's plan for you?

Just as Naomi found her way back to the God of Israel, so God taught me to walk beyond my wilderness. It was God alone who gave me courage to face what was to come.

Chapter 12

Returning to Leadership

*Significant character development occurs as God
redeems leaders from their mistakes.*
—Henry and Richard Blackaby

I f you ever desired to get back into relationship with God
after turning your back on him, you know that returning to him is one of the most freeing experiences you will enjoy.
However, if you ever wanted to return to the church after an extended time away, you know it can be one of the most terrifying
experiences you will endure. Compound that with leadership and
feeling like a colossal failure, and you may find the weight almost
unbearable.

When Judas betrayed Christ, he felt only failure. He saw no
way out and couldn't live with himself. Conversely, when Simon
Peter denied Christ, he, too, knew he'd failed, but his story wrote
a different ending. The joy and love he experienced while learning
from Jesus over three years may have seemed a total loss to him
until something amazing happened.

According to John 21:1–17, after Jesus's crucifixion and resurrection, he appeared to his disciples a third time. It was John, the beloved disciple, who first recognized him. But when Jesus invited the group to come in from their fishing boats and have breakfast by a warm fire on the beach, it was Peter who hauled in a net full of fish and brought it to Jesus. Then it happened—the part of the story that is, to me, the most amazing and significant.

After they finished breakfast, Jesus asked a question. "Peter, son of John, do you love me more than these?" It had only been a few days since Peter denied Jesus three times, yet here was Jesus asking Peter a question—three times, no less. Each time Peter affirmed his love, Jesus responded with: "Feed my lambs," "Tend my sheep," and "Feed my sheep."

I can't help but wonder what went through Peter's mind in those moments. Did he understand what Jesus was saying to him? Was he frustrated? Did he wonder if Jesus was repeating the same question because his answers weren't good enough? Was he upset because he thought Jesus wasn't taking him seriously? Was the impact of what Jesus was asking sinking into his heart and soul?

Scripture doesn't tell us what went through Peter's mind, but it says he grieved. Maybe he felt sad because he thought Jesus wasn't sure he could trust him any longer. Maybe he thought Jesus didn't believe him or thought his responses weren't authentic.

I can imagine how Peter may have felt. When we make our way out of a dark wilderness, our confidence is shaky. We're on guard. We wonder if the circles of ministry and friends where we once thrived will accept us. Will they trust us? Will they invite us back to do the things that once brought us joy? This story of Peter and Jesus on the beach gives us hope that, just maybe, our life is worth something. That we are still of some use.

Jesus knew Peter was remorseful and chose this setting, this venue, this time, to reaffirm God's call on Peter's life. Yes! He was commissioning Peter back into ministry.

As I was making my way out of my fifteen-year wilderness and trying to work out where I fit within the church, I believe God gave me this story to cling to in the early phases of my journey. He wanted me to know that my wilderness period did not negate his calling on my life or eliminate me from stepping back into leadership. He began a good work in me and would bring it to completion at the day of Jesus Christ (Philippians 1:6). Just as he recommissioned Peter to ministry, so he was calling me back to some form of ministry, though I didn't know at the time what it would be.

Returning to leadership is not a now you're in, now you're out, now you're back in, kind of scenario. It takes courage, humility, accountability, and intentionality. And a lot of forgiveness all around.

Being Courageous

"Be strong, and let your heart take courage, all you who wait for the LORD" (Psalm 31:24).

After my grandma immigrated to Canada in 1928, it took her forty years before she returned to England to visit family and friends. Her long delay was partially because of a worldwide depression, a world war, deaths of her two husbands, a miscarriage, and raising her daughter as a single mom—not to mention the cost of undertaking a trip that seemed like a luxury. But something more debilitating lay beneath her reluctance to undertake such a journey.

Though Grandma originally arrived in Canada onboard a ship, she knew that if she were to return to England for a visit, it would have to be by plane. But whenever she referred to flying, there was a veiled hesitancy in her voice. Fear kept raising its head.

I always saw my grandma's life as one that required bravery to survive and courage to stand strong. And she did just that. I never saw her back down from anything without a good reason. She knew the meaning of "discretion is the better part of valor." But the idea of flying in a plane demanded more than she seemed able to muster. Fear threatened to rob her of something she longed to do.

On the day she told me she'd booked a flight to England, I remember her seeming to rationalize her decision.

"When your time is up, it's up," she explained. "It doesn't matter if you're in an airplane or walking down the street." She was right.

What must have been a deep inner struggle became a lesson for her and an example to me. Though I was sixteen at the time, Grandma showed me what growth through inner struggle looked like. She and God worked through her inner fear and came to a resolve that seemed to deepen her relationship with him.

Grandma witnessed God's hand on her life through more sorrow and disappointment than some people face in a lifetime. This was simply one more opportunity to place her confidence in him and face the fear that had stalked her for years. It was a giant step of faith. She truly believed God had a hold of her, no matter where she was. By her example, she taught me never to let anything hold me back out of fear, because fear robs and destroys.

Yes, returning to leadership after a fall can conjure up all kinds of fears and keep us from fulfilling God's call in our lives. We wonder what people will say or think. *Will they trust me? What if I fall again? Will they be waiting for me to fall again?*

But that's exactly where the devil wants us. Right there in the middle of defeat. He has no desire for us to step back into relationship with God and the work he has for us to accomplish. He wants us to go through life, caught up in the opposite of courage—being afraid, timid, doubtful, insecure, defeated. However, "God has not given us a spirit of fear and timidity, but of power, love, and self-discipline" (2 Timothy 1:7 NLT).

As we step out and away from what has bound us up, we, by God's grace, become overcomers with renewed purpose. Just as

God recommissioned Peter to serve, so we may step into God's renewed call on our lives. That said, Peter cautions us to "Stay alert! Watch out for your great enemy, the devil. He prowls around like a roaring lion, looking for someone to devour" (1 Peter 5:8 NLT). Peter, from his own experience, also reminds us in the closing chapter of 2 Peter that the Lord "does not want anyone to be destroyed, but wants everyone to repent" (2 Peter 3:9 NLT).

Being Humble

"Clothe yourselves, all of you, with humility toward one another, for God opposes the proud but gives grace to the humble" (1 Peter 5:5).

Biographies are one of my favorite genres to read. I'm challenged and inspired by the lives of those who went on before us and the strength they showed in adversity and victory. Whether these books recount the achievements of Christian men or women from the Middle Ages or the exploits of lives lived in latter centuries, each story reveals qualities that stand firm in obedience to God's call. Those who lived long lives and those who died young. Those who received accolades and those who were falsely accused. Writers. Preachers. Teachers. Mothers. Missionaries. Each one exhibited a level of humility that did not silence them. It emboldened them.

People like Anne Askew (1521–1546), who suffered unimaginable torture before they burned her broken body at the stake as a heretic. She was only twenty-five years of age. She never wavered as she took her stand on the Word of God and the conviction that Scripture, not man, was the ultimate authority.[9]

Then there was Phillis Wheatley (1753–1784), who suffered the horrors of slavery and the humiliation of being considered less than human. Though she was a gifted poet, she died alone and in poverty. Yet she never stopped praising God for his kindness, goodness, and mercy.[10]

Edith Stein (1891–1942) was the youngest of eleven children

in a devout Jewish family, but she abandoned her faith. She became a recognized educator and later dedicated herself completely to God and to writing while serving others as a nun. When Nazis came for her and her sister, she quietly surrendered her life.[11]

Countless stories of faithful Christians challenge us to obediently and humbly bend, not to man, but to the will of God and his definitive call on our lives. Yet, our greatest example of humility is Jesus himself when, "being found in human form, he humbled himself by becoming obedient to the point of death, even death on a cross" (Philippians 2:8). As Jesus washed his disciples' feet—a task that was considered lowly servant work—he showed us how we are to be toward one another (John 13:3–15). But more importantly, he sacrificed himself on the cross for our sins—an authentic example of humility.

Being Accountable

"Search me, O God, and know my heart! Try me and know my thoughts! And see if there be any grievous way in me, and lead me in the way everlasting" (Psalm 139:23–24).

One of the hardest things for us humans to learn is to admit when we're wrong or that we made a mistake. It hurts our pride—and some of us can be quite prideful. But as Proverbs 16:18 tells us, "Pride goes before destruction, and a haughty spirit before a fall."

Many lone rangers meet their demise because they refuse to be accountable. They think they know better than the people appointed to guide them. Countless movies and books depict the protagonist as a maverick who falls flat on his face until he listens to instruction. Athletic stars and gifted musicians fail until they realize they don't know better than their coaches. Great empires crumble when kings or dictators refuse to listen to wise advisers. Enterprises go bankrupt or split apart because business owners say, "I'll do it my way" rather than hold themselves accountable to shareholders or a board of directors.

But what about Christian leadership and accountability? Scripture instructs us to love one another. Isn't accountability wrapped up in that "love one another" directive? Doesn't God require us "to do justice, and to love kindness, and to walk humbly with our God" (Micah 6:8)? Did Jesus not submit and hold himself accountable to the Father when he prayed, "My Father, if it be possible, let this cup pass from me; nevertheless, not as I will, but as you will." (Matthew 26:39)?

Submitting ourselves to be accountable to another person or to a governing body is difficult, especially when we think they're wrong. But if we are to grow in the grace and knowledge of our Lord Jesus Christ and excel in the work God laid out for us, we must have ears to hear and eyes to see. We must be teachable and accountable.

Just as Barnabas mentored Paul, and Paul discipled Timothy, God places people in our lives to instruct us in our growth as leaders. Does that mean we don't question or disagree? Absolutely not. Blindly receiving what someone else says has led many Christians down the wrong path. Instead, we must dig into the Word for ourselves. We must evaluate what we read and hear against what God says. We must weigh the advice and teaching of others against the wisdom and instruction found in the Word of God. He brings people into our lives to guide and instruct us. Yet, he is also the One to whom we are ultimately accountable.

Being teachable and studying the Bible to learn what God says about what someone said or wrote is one form of accountability. It's being accountable to "Do your best to present yourself to God as one approved, a worker who has no need to be ashamed, rightly handling the word of truth" (2 Timothy 2:15).

Another form of accountability comes into play when we realize we made a mistake or we're confronted by someone who believes we made a mistake. In the natural, the temptation is to deny it or make excuses or shift the blame to circumstances or someone else. My dog ate my homework or my computer died, or, or, or . . . In reality, however, it was still my mistake.

In my lifetime, I've made many mistakes. And some of them have been of epic proportions. Do I still make mistakes? Sadly, yes. But, along the way, I've learned that when I accept responsibility for those mistakes, other people become empowered and grow. If my mistake affects a team of people and I sincerely apologize for it, the team emerges stronger. As leaders, we need to admit our mistake, apologize to those involved, offer a solution if possible, and move on. It becomes a teachable moment for us and everyone involved.

Running away from mistakes we make—whether real or imagined—is not an option. Okay, yes, it's an option. But it's not a wise choice for leaders who have the desire for God to use them.

David could have run away when Nathan confronted him about the mountain of mistakes he'd made as king. But he didn't. In 2 Samuel 12:13, we read that David said, "I have sinned against the Lord." He admitted his mistakes and, in Psalm 51, begs God to have mercy on him. He further asks God in verses 10–12 to, "Create in me a clean heart, O God, and renew a right spirit within me. Cast me not away from your presence, and take not your Holy Spirit from me. Restore to me the joy of your salvation, and uphold me with a willing spirit."

Being Intentional

"Do not be conformed to this world, but be transformed by the renewal of your mind, that by testing you may discern what is the will of God, what is good and acceptable and perfect" (Romans 12:2).

On October 27, 1999, in the middle of my desert wilderness, I penned this entry into my journal:

I wish I could take back those black, foreboding times in my life where good was at war with evil, where white and black struggled in gray.

At the time of that writing, I was trying to find my way out of darkness. Trying to find peace in uncertainty. And trying to make sense of my journey.

On one occasion, I went to the cemetery and sat on the grass by Grandma's grave. It was a sunny day with a light breeze rustling the leaves of the nearby tree. And it was peaceful. I knew she wasn't there and couldn't hear me, but I talked out loud anyway.

"Grandma, I made such a mess of things. I'm so sorry for failing and bringing dishonor to what you lived for and what you taught me. Your life was a life of sacrifice and unconditional love. I want to be like you." And then I added, "God, help me."

They were heartfelt words that only he heard. But they were a beginning. They were intentional.

Throughout history, people called out to God in desperation. They hung on to the end of a rope that was about to give way under the tension, and screamed, "God! Help!"

People like the woman we read about in Genesis, chapters 16 and 21. When Abraham and Sarah banished Hagar to the wilderness of Beersheba, she ran out of water, laid her son under a tree, and wept. She couldn't bear to watch her son die of exposure and thirst. She reached what she thought was the end and cried. But God saw her. He comforted and provided for her and told her what to do next. And with great intention, she did what he told her.

Many stories have been told of missionaries who made choices that seemed unreasonable to others. Intentionally, they ventured into uncharted and hazardous areas or embarked on dangerous missions to take the gospel to people who would otherwise not hear it. To many people, they were brave—even heroes. To others, they were foolish or reckless. Yet, their firm belief in God's call on their lives caused them to step out in faith. They intentionally followed God's leading, no matter where it led.

How many of us are in that league of intentional followers?

If we believe God has called and gifted us to lead, regardless of where that may be, we must be purposeful in how we live our lives. We must intentionally spend time with him and read his Word. And we must intentionally love unconditionally.

It's easy to get so busy with activity that our relationship with God suffers. We miss taking time to be quiet with the Lord. His best gets lost as we neglect to focus on him. We become deaf to what he's trying to tell us or blind to what he's trying to show us.

As we grow in courage, humility, accountability, and intentionality, we grow as leaders. Yet that growth is not a now-I've-learned-it-so-let's-move-on kind of scenario. Leadership, with its failures and victories, carries on through life. Our learning is never over. We stumble. We get back up. We run the race. And all the while we're held by the reality of God's grace and unending love for those he chose.

As I made my way back into church and leadership, inner whispers often plagued my thoughts. *Who do you think you are?* Or, *You wandered away once; what makes you think it won't happen again?* It was in those tormenting times that Isaiah 41:9–10 gave me confidence to press on:

"You are my servant, I have chosen you and not cast you off; fear not, for I am with you; be not dismayed, for I am your God; I will strengthen you, I will help you, I will uphold you with my righteous right hand."

God used those words to assure me he had rescued me by his grace and empowered me with his strength to venture into what was, to me, the unknown. It became a passage I returned to time and time again as I continued in my journey back.

Part 4

RESTORED TO SERVE

The faithfulness of God, wrapped
in his enduring love and amazing grace.

Chapter 13

Invited to Lead

Let us never forget that what we are
is more important than what we do.
—J. Hudson Taylor

Following the conference in March 2005, where I played the drums and had a couple of *aha* moments, I spent a full year digging deep and wide into what was happening in churches and ministries. I talked with people I knew and people I met for the first time. I devoured books, magazines, and internet articles like a moth at a wool convention. And I had fun. I was discovering a renewed energy. A fresh passion was building within me. And I wanted more. Yet I had the sense I was to do exactly what I was doing—simply explore and listen, for now.

Ideas percolated, so I wrote them down for safekeeping. I did not know where they might go or how God would use them. It seemed he was preparing me for a big adventure. I just needed to rest and let him unfold the plan in his time. Strangely enough, I felt content to do just that. Then the red and amber lights of stop and slow turned green. Go.

On May 8, 2006, I received an email asking if I would consider taking on the leadership of women's ministries at the church we were attending. My first thought was, if they only knew where I'd been and what I'd done. The invitation intrigued me, but I was cautious when I responded.

"I don't know what to say because I haven't been thinking along those lines. What are you looking for in a leader?"

Almost immediately another email arrived in my inbox, saying they thought I was the one God had for the job and outlined what they were looking for. The person had to be someone who could give leadership—someone with a vision and a passion and the ability to communicate it.

Between the email exchanges and sitting down together over coffee the next evening, I wondered if this was the direction God was sending me. To be sure, however, I said I needed time to consider the invitation and would get back to them at the end of the month. I wanted to talk with the lead pastor to be certain I'd have the support of the church leadership and freedom to use the first year to connect with the women to determine needs. Based on what I learned over my year of digging into churches and their ministries to women, it seemed to be time for a new model. I believed it wasn't about programs. It had to be about people. About connection and relationships. And that required a lot of listening.

For those of us who are Type A personalities or "git 'er done" drivers, it's difficult to say, "I need some time before I give my answer." Our first thought is to jump (with a basic plan, of course) and sort everything out along the way. It's hard to take a breath before plowing ahead into what we see as an exciting venture. But that's exactly what I knew I needed to do—pray about it, talk to people I respected for their wisdom and discernment, and evaluate the implications on my life. After all, I was still getting my feet on solid ground after a long wilderness trek away from the church.

I already had a lot of activities on my calendar. As primary breadwinner in our home, I needed to be sure my coaching business continued to do well. I enjoyed playing on the church worship team, serving on a couple of community boards, reading, writing, and spending time with friends and family. I loved the balance I had gained in my life since our move from the city, and I wanted to keep it.

As I prayed and processed, I talked with people who had known me for many years. They were supportive and spurred me on with their insights.

My friend Faith, who was on the Women's Ministries of Canada national board with me in the 1980s, talked about how we had both experienced the death of a vision but that it's sometimes necessary to redefine and relaunch in order to rebuild.

Eileen, who had mentored me in my early leadership years and was with me when my grandma died, said, "We need new muscle and new teeth because our muscle has become soft and our teeth have fallen out. But be sure that whatever you do, it is Word centered."

My friend Lillian, who had a knack for bringing new perspectives to most discussions, knew I was looking beyond the local church to a broader ministry. She encouraged me by saying, "If a new model is to be developed, it needs to be transferable to other groups." She then recommended that if I accept the church role I "consider the existing women's activities and what they need to sustain themselves, so they don't feel orphaned while you evaluate and plan."

Besides the friends that I talked with, I also created a short list of questions to run by the pastor before asking them of each church board and staff member and others in leadership. Questions like: What did they see as the three-year vision for the church? Was it written anywhere? What role did the ministry of women currently play in fulfilling that vision? How can we better equip, challenge, empower, and support women at the church to ensure they're actively involved in fulfilling the vision?

I knew from experience that to build something, one did not have to destroy the foundation. The women of the church had been very active in the past and were still engaged. But I believed it wasn't about filling women's time or finding them things to do. It was about connecting them to God and to each other. It was about helping them identify their giftedness, providing them with support and encouragement, and challenging and equipping them to fulfill God's plan for them.

After meeting with the pastor, my husband and I invited him and his wife to meet us in our home. I believed if I was to take on a leadership role, I needed to be transparent with the lead pastor about what had happened during my wilderness wanderings. Jim agreed and sat next to me as I briefly recounted my journey. Was it easy? Absolutely not. But they were very gracious and assured me of their support. The pastor also said he didn't think that what I told them had to go any further.

Before giving my definitive answer, I wanted to talk with my daughter, Sarah. Over the years, her God-given gifts of wisdom and discernment were obvious. She had also seen my journey up close and personal. As we walked around the neighborhood, I filled her in on the invitation I'd received, the decision I had to make within a day or two, and where I was in my thinking. Settling on a bench at the nearby park, we continued our conversation.

"I know I'm no Moses," I began, "but I feel a bit like he must have felt when God met him at the burning bush, told him to leave the desert where he'd been living, and commissioned him to go to Egypt and lead his people."

Sarah listened intently as I rambled on. Finally, she said, "Mom, God is leading you back to your Egypt." Then she quickly added, "I'm not saying the church is Egypt, but I am saying I believe God is leading you back to where he had you serving before your wilderness."

I've never forgotten those words: "God is leading you back to *your* Egypt."

Sometimes, God puts us in reverse to move us forward, as if to say, *It's time to go back to where we left off and build from there.*

My notes from that three-week period of decision-making included a list of pros and cons and a personal time and needs assessment. I asked myself questions like: Is this where God wants me to serve? What are the immediate and long-term consequences of my saying yes? What if I say, "No. Never?" What if I say, "Not this year?" I also broke down my current activities and how much time they each required and did some serious praying and reading. It was important to be absolutely sure before stepping into the role.

A roller coaster of emotions took me from being excited at the potential to being afraid of its bigness. I felt overwhelmed at how everything would fit together and how I'd keep up with my coaching business. Would this opportunity pull me away from the passion God was reigniting in me or was it part of it?

In the final analysis, at the bottom of my notes, I wrote, "Calm. Peace. Logical." The combination of everything I processed and prayed through made total sense. I said yes.

A month after the initial email invitation, I attended the congregation's annual general meeting and met with the church women to listen to their ideas and share what I envisioned for the coming year. Having been out of ministry for so long, I couldn't help but think about Nehemiah when he was called by God to rebuild the walls of Jerusalem. Like him, I prayed and listened—a lot. But unlike Nehemiah, I escaped to the beach with my friend Bev.

After a demanding month, I believed God had given me a vision for the work ahead and a passion to move forward. But I needed some quiet time. For the next few days at our friend's beach house, Bev and I enjoyed catching up with each other while we soaked in the sea breeze and warm sunshine. Our friendship was one that didn't always need our voices to be heard. We were equally content to enjoy conversation and share silence. It was the perfect place to pray, read, and consider next steps.

A few days earlier, I'd thought about what to look for in potential team members. The brief list included qualities like: a desire to honor God out of love for him, a heart of concern for others, a walk that matched their talk, a motivation to explore new ideas and think outside the box, a desire to mature in their faith, and the willingness to work and be teachable. But who were these women?

With my list of qualities in hand, I now sat at the beach and prayed, "Okay, Lord, here's the list. Help me know who will make up this team of women leaders."

This may seem strange, but as I rested my pen on the paper, God literally planted seven names in my mind, and I jotted them down in order. A couple of them were women I knew fairly well, a couple were women I'd occasionally talked with, and the others were women I knew only by reputation.

Over the next two weeks, I met with each one. After asking them to tell me about their spiritual journey, I told them what I believed God was leading me to do and that their name was on "the list." Would they prayerfully consider being part of a women's leadership team?

As I listened to their stories, I realized God had pulled together a team of wounded warriors. Each one of us carried scars we'd received in God's battle for our lives and stood only because of his grace. As warriors, we were learning daily how to draw on the power of his divine weapons. Each of us wanted to grow in our relationship with God, connect with and help others on their journeys, and lead women closer to the heart of God. At the end of the two weeks, every one of the seven—ranging in ages from early thirties up to late sixties—agreed to join the team. And what a team they became.

Throughout the summer, we studied, prayed, worked on team

building, and looked to God for where he wanted us to grow the ministry. We conducted a survey of all the women of the church, went on an overnight strategic planning time, and came away unified in our vision to "connect and equip women to live authentic, transforming lives and to communicate God's love and hope to women across cultural and generational boundaries."

Just as Nehemiah followed God's call to rebuild the walls of Jerusalem, so I believed he called me to work with an amazing team of women whom he handpicked. I believed women needed to be encouraged to grow spiritually. That they needed to be challenged to discover and develop their God-given gifts and presented with opportunities to exercise them. They needed to become confident in their strengths so they could fulfill God's plan for them. And I firmly believed it had to start with the leadership team—meeting them where they were in their journey—connecting heart to heart with each other and heart to heart with God.

In those days, I came to love the Old Testament book of Nehemiah and continued to go back to it often. It's full of leadership principles we can draw on as we seek to fulfill God's call in our lives.

First, we see in Nehemiah 1:1–3, that Nehemiah asked travelers how things were going for the men and women who escaped the exile and were living in Jerusalem. But why should he care? As cupbearer to King Artaxerxes, Nehemiah had it pretty good in the king's courts. He was comfortable and held a respected job that garnered the king's trust. Yes, it could be a dangerous occupation if someone wanted to poison the king, but God placed Nehemiah there for a greater purpose. His curiosity to know what was happening almost 900 miles away tells me God was already working in Nehemiah to prepare him for what lay ahead. And God still does that today.

Has God placed you somewhere that's fairly comfortable, but

he's now stirring a passion within you to do something you never considered before? Have you been mulling something over or asking questions and digging for more information on an issue? Could it be that God is placing a desire within you to do a new thing?

Second, when Nehemiah learned what was happening in Jerusalem, he was so affected by it he wept and mourned for days while he fasted and prayed and asked for God's guidance (Nehemiah 1:4–11).

When God arouses a passion in us, and we dwell on what we learn by asking questions and studying, we can become overwhelmed by it all. We can experience brain overload and become muddled in our thinking. Or we can become so moved by what we learn that we're carried away with emotion. Like Nehemiah, we must lay it all before God and trust him to sort it out. He will give us wisdom to make the right decisions and will make our path straight (Proverbs 3:5–6).

Third, Nehemiah was bold in his answers when the king asked, "What are you requesting?"

But notice how Nehemiah didn't rely on his own ability to provide the best answer. Instead, Nehemiah 2:4 tells us that before he opened his mouth to respond, he "prayed to the God of heaven."

As leaders, we don't have all the answers perfectly lined up. Sometimes we jump first and pray later, only to find that we jumped over a cliff. Nehemiah gives us a good leadership principle to follow—pray first.

Fourth, I believe we can conclude that Nehemiah was proactive. He did his research and had a skeleton plan in mind before he approached the king. He took all his apprehension and concerns to God and came away with newfound courage and inspiration. Out of his days of praying and fasting, Nehemiah knew what he needed for his mission to Jerusalem. He didn't just shoot up a quick prayer and leave it at that. He prayed for days, prior to the king asking why he looked so sad. And before he gave his response, he shot up a sentence prayer. Nehemiah was constantly in a state of prayer.

When God plants a passion within us, he doesn't expect us to sit back and just think about it. He expects us to lay it all before him and get moving. Stepping out, to move forward, is a choice. And stepping in to where God is calling us takes courage.

Fifth, when Nehemiah finally made it to Jerusalem, Nehemiah 2:11 seems to suggest that he rested for three days. After his rest, verses 12–16 tell us he went by himself, under the cover of night, to survey the situation. I can almost see Nehemiah stumbling around in the rubble, trying to find his way in the dark, before he finally sat on a jagged rock, rested his head in his hands, and said, "God, this is *huge*." As he sat there thinking about all the work that lay ahead, he prayed and prepared the next phase of the plan to rebuild the walls.

When we're called to fulfill a special God mission, our hearts and minds need to be continually praying and researching. It's not a one-time-only prayer or a master plan set in concrete. God doesn't always give us the entire plan all at once. Often, he unfolds it as we put one foot in front of the other—even if we sometimes have to step over jagged rocks.

Sixth, as if the people weren't already able to see the surrounding devastation, Nehemiah pointed out the dire straits they were in and emphasized the negative impact it was having on their reputation (Nehemiah 2:17). He then told his own story of what God had done in his life, how he led him to Jerusalem, and why he was there. As a result, people joined Nehemiah's team and said, "Let us rise up and build" (Nehemiah 2:18).

Just as Nehemiah's story made a difference to the people in Jerusalem, so our stories matter to people around us. When we tell them what God is doing in our lives, it encourages and challenges them on their own life journeys. When we acknowledge where we've been and where we are now, people can become motivated to fulfill God's purpose for their lives.

Finally, Nehemiah knew it was God who would cause them to succeed and that he couldn't fulfill God's plan by himself. Nehemiah 2:20 tells us, "The God of heaven will make us prosper." That's dependence on God for the outcome. The verse also says, "and we his servants will arise and build." That's recognizing it takes a team to accomplish a mission. Chapter 3 lists all the households who stepped up to the work. Men and women alike were involved in the repairs and rebuilding. It was a big team.

Sometimes, we as leaders become so focused on fulfilling the plan and achieving the goal that we forget it's not about us or deadlines or what we can do. It's about the growth of the team God put together to work with us. It's about the work he's doing in each team member while achieving the mission.

Marked in the margin of my Bible, beside Colossians 1:10, are the words, "M.M.B.I. 1969/70." Years ago in Bible school, that verse was real to me. "Walk in a manner worthy of the Lord, fully pleasing to him: bearing fruit in every good work and increasing in the knowledge of God." Sadly, that reality waned in my life.

Years later, I marked Colossians 4:17 with the date April 2007. It was the verse God gave me to hold on to as I made my way out of the wilderness, rediscovered the richness of his Word, and wondered if he could ever use me again after I had made a royal mess of things. The verse reads, "See that you fulfill the ministry that you have received in the Lord."

Today, both verses stand out as a picture of God's grace and call on a life. God calls us. God never lets us go. And God invites us to be restored to serve.

In the coming year, I would cling to those verses in the middle of a whole lot of messiness.

Chapter 14

On Trial

Can you thank Me for trusting you with this experience,
even if I never tell you why?
—Helen Roseveare

"What? This can't be right." I dropped to the couch to read the report again.

Almost three years had passed since I accepted the invitation to get back into church leadership. Every step was one of growth for me as pastor of women and the seven women serving with me on the leadership team. We melded in a way I had never seen a team come together. Though the moment-by-moment connection of texting wasn't yet a thing, whenever we saw each other, it was as if we'd been talking every day.

In January 2007, just six months into my new role, I drove to our regular women's leadership team meeting. My schedule was full with church ministry, coaching business, and writing and teaching a weekly Growing Women Leaders workshop series in the community. I loved meeting with the team, but during that short drive, I felt sad and overwhelmed, which wasn't like me at all. I struggled with the thought that I didn't have enough inside me to fulfill all my responsibilities.

As darkness threatened to overtake me, I heard my heart say, "Focus on God," and I sang:

> Praise God from whom all blessings flow.
> Praise him all creatures here below.
> Praise him above ye heavenly hosts.
> Praise Father, Son, and Holy Ghost.[12]

When I arrived, I sat in the car for a few minutes before heading into the meeting. We each found a place at the oversized dining room table. One in our group shared a short devotional before I asked, "So, how's everyone doing—really? How can we best pray for each other?"

Silence.

Slowly, one by one, team members shared bits of what was happening in their lives and where they needed prayer. As each one spoke up, a heaviness seemed to fill the room. Everyone in their own way expressed feelings of being stressed and overwhelmed. Serious health issues. Unsettling family concerns. Lack of focus and order. And so on.

I sat, taking it all in. Everyone was in the same dark place I'd felt on my way here. How could this be happening? This amazing team had accomplished so much over these past months. We were seeing lives changed. What was going on?

As the heaviness continued to fill the room, Donna, the eldest of the group, spoke up, "When things like this happen, it's often just before God is going to do something big. And our enemy doesn't like it one bit."

As I looked around the table, women nodded but didn't make eye contact.

"Satan knows how to get to each of us," I began. "He wants to throw us off track. We need to trust God in those times so we can keep going."

Joining hands, we prayed God would bind the enemy and use us to do the work he'd called us to. We also committed to pray for one another intentionally in the coming weeks. The transformation was incredible.

As we continued down the agenda items, it was clear God was working. Three-quarters of the way through the meeting, I spotted our youngest member—my daughter, Sarah—smiling as she methodically scanned the table and looked into the face of each woman.

"What is it, Sarah?" I asked.

"Oh, I'm just noticing the difference around the table. When we began tonight, everyone looked stressed and sad. Now everyone is smiling and excited. Ideas are popping up all over the place."

We closed the meeting unusually late that evening. No one seemed ready to leave. Everyone lingered to talk and spontaneously set one-on-one meetings with each other. That night, I came away with renewed hope and excitement, reminded that God is greater than anything we might face.

In the following two years, the ministry thrived. While we continued to build on activities that functioned prior to my arrival, we also worked together to develop new ways to reach women. Two significant initiatives especially stand out in my mind.

It was Saturday morning, May 2007. My cell phone rang, so I slipped out of a meeting to take the call. As I leaned against the wall in a downstairs section of the church, my eyes fell on a mountain of chaos. Broken furniture, stacks of paper, and discarded equipment covered the height and depth of this secluded alcove in the farthest corner of the building. As I talked on the phone and surveyed the scene in front of me, I saw beyond the confusion and into the possibilities. This mess could be a life-giving space.

Within the next few days, the women's leadership team met and quickly caught the vision when I recounted the picture I believed God had painted in my mind. As we prayed and strategized about the purpose for the space, we agreed the project would provide an inviting and relaxing, adult-friendly room where men and women of the church and community could connect with Jesus and each other. We also discussed the practical and creative skills we needed to accomplish the renovations and who we could enlist to help.

It would not be a simple task, but the potential got us excited, and Cindy, one of our team, agreed to oversee the work. The next step was to write a proposal and get the approval of the church board, which we did. Within a month, reclamation got into full swing with junk removal and repairs, electrical work, painting, and construction of a wall with a door to make it an enclosed room— all under Cindy's creative supervision. The unsightly alcove soon transformed into what felt like someone's living room, with a serving counter for beverages and snacks.

Since opening in September 2007, the room has hosted group gatherings and Bible studies, and has been a place to stop in and talk with someone. Evenings when kids' clubs were running, hosts welcomed parents who dropped in for fellowship and a warm drink while waiting for their children.

As we neared the completion of our "room" project, a series of events unfolded for another initiative. This one, however, would stretch us beyond our comfort zones.

It was a Sunday morning when I first met Edith, a missionary who was home on furlough and staying with our mutual friend, Donna, who had served with Edith. We immediately connected.

"Edith, do you ever have teams come to your field to help on a short-term basis?" I blurted.

Where did that come from? I wondered, as my voice jumped ahead of my brain.

When Edith declared, "Yes. Absolutely," we both knew we had to talk further, and arranged a meeting for later that day.

Sitting in Donna's living room, Edith told me about the work she was involved in, and we discussed the potential of taking a team of women to the small country she served.

A couple hours into our conversation, and with the number ten in my mind, I asked, "What would be a good number of women to bring?"

"Ten," she responded. And with that, the wheels kicked into motion.

By Christmas, ten women ranging in age from nineteen to six-ty-nine committed to being part of a team to travel to an island country in the West Indies. Together, we were to minister alongside resident, full-time missionaries. But raising funds and preparing the team for a cross-cultural venture was key.

From January through April, two teams came together and got to work—the "go team" and the "stay team." The "go team" met regularly for team building. We prayed together, dug into the Word, learned about the country we'd see and people we'd meet, and received training in cross-cultural ministry from Donna and a retired missionary friend who taught missions at the nearby sem-inary. The "stay team" was comprised of women unable to travel with us but who committed themselves to the vital roles of prayer warrior and support. Meanwhile, the rest of the church soon caught the buzz and joined in on the fundraising efforts.

On April 28, 2008, a healthy team of ten women left home, excited at what lay ahead. But by the time we arrived at the air-port an hour later, I had come down with an instant, full-blown head and chest cold that sapped all my energy for most of our six-teen-day trip. No doubt it was God's way of reminding me he put us together and would fulfill his purpose, even if I was sick.

Though we didn't all know each other when we'd first met

together five months earlier, by the time we set out for the airport, we cared for one another and appreciated each individual's strengths. During our travels, we each had a job. Eileen became our go-to, first-aid person, and official photographer. Shelley, an experienced globe-trotting travel agent, took care of travel and customs issues. Donna, the eldest, assumed the role of "mom" to the team and nursed me through some rough days so I could fulfill my speaking and leadership roles. Everyone on the team sang, performed dramas, played an instrument, shared testimonies, or taught.

Thankfully, no one else got sick on the trip. We carried on with our full itinerary of performing music and drama concerts, teaching workshops and leadership seminars, coming alongside women, and traveling the island country to sit with local believers. God blessed and stretched us beyond our comfort zones, as people came to the Lord and believers were encouraged. It was pure joy.

After our return on May 13, we hosted a lunch for our church family to thank them for their support and to report on the outcomes of the trip. The whole church praised God for the great things he had done and looked forward to the coming ministry year.

One month later, I received an email from a senior church staff member followed by a report written and circulated by him to the church board and staff. Reading the report and email, my chest tightened. Though I wanted to scream, I craved stillness. I had the urge to fight but wanted to cry in defeat. I longed to go full speed ahead but wanted to quit.

This can't be right. I sat on the couch and read, "the women's ministries team is the most disconnected from vision, direction, and methodology of the church," and "they operate independently of the church ministry team."

How can this be? I felt like someone had kicked me in the chest. The comments were calling our ministry and leadership integrity into question.

But why? Hadn't God blessed this team? Didn't the results show he was in it? The congregation supported various initiatives we presented and worked with us toward the same end. This had to be a misunderstanding.

The next week, I received a call telling me not to attend the staff meeting the next day when the report was to be discussed. This made no sense at all. Why would the leader of a ministry negatively singled out not be present to discuss next steps with the rest of the staff with whom she'd been serving?

"Don't take the comments personally," I was told by the report writer.

But I did—not just for me, but for my entire team. I expressed my concern that unsubstantiated conclusions, made by one person with influence, threatened to derail a ministry that saw lives changed for Christ and demoralize a dedicated team. But the decision was made. My objections went unheeded. I was not to attend the meeting.

Two days later, I met with the person responsible for the report and was asked if I agreed with it. When I said I couldn't, I was told my position on staff was in jeopardy.

Because I believed the situation could be resolved, I didn't yet think it necessary to share the report with the women's team. But despite emails, phone calls, and volunteering to meet with the church board to discuss concerns or questions, I felt nothing was being done to determine the truth or untruth of the report's conclusions. It was becoming difficult to know where I stood, and I thought it unfair for the women's leadership team not to be aware of the report summary.

Almost two months after circulation of the report, I talked with the board chair, who did not object to my talking about the report with the women's team. That night, I shared comments written about the women's ministries team, then watched and listened as they absorbed what I was reading. They initially reacted with humanness, but they didn't stay there long. Shock, sadness, and even a little anger quickly changed to concern, peace, and determination to be vigilant in prayer and to what God had called us to do. Thankfulness for each one of them and for what God had done in our lives overwhelmed me. There was a definite sense of God's presence.

Another two weeks passed. Again, I received a call to meet with the report writer, which I did. He wanted to know if I had changed my mind and would now agree with what he wrote in the report.

"I'm sorry. I cannot agree because the conclusions are not true."

"Well then, based on your response, I can no longer consider you on staff," he replied. "I can't work with someone who doesn't agree with me."

Working hard to keep my composure, I replied, "Regardless of what happens to me, I believe it's important for the women's team to meet with you to talk about the issues in the report."

But he declined.

The next day, I contacted the church board chair to request a meeting between the women's leadership team and the board, so they could hear from the team and collectively work toward a resolution regarding the issues that had come out of this situation. To me, this was the next step in following the process laid out in Matthew 18.

About three weeks later, I received a call from the church office to arrange a meeting of the women's leadership team with the report writer. By this time, it had been determined by church leadership that the process used to come to the report conclusions was flawed. However, despite this determination and spending two hours with the women's team, the report writer stood by his conclusions.

In September 2008, three and a half months after the report had been released, a meeting was scheduled for the church board, women's leadership team, and staff. It was to be our opportunity to present the concerns we had about the report and enable everyone to come together to reconcile the situation and move forward. Though guarded, I was hopeful. I believed that the paralyzing accusations leveled against me and the team would find resolution.

When I entered the meeting room, the board members were seated behind long tables set up along one wall. The staff and women's leadership team sat in a semi-circle facing the church board, with a single chair at one end designated for me.

After a reading of the brief I'd previously submitted in writing, questions came up about why I'd been let go from the staff. From there, the meeting spiraled downward. And then the final blow came.

"I don't trust her and can't work with someone I can't trust. She's not a team player."

As words spilled from my accuser's mouth, gasps of disbelief came from people in the room who knew me well. I was stunned but sat still, responding only when asked specific questions.

My heart felt stomped on. Yet concern for my team grew. They faced the whole volatile situation with grace and courage but were hurting. Tears were on the faces of some of the team, and Sarah—our youngest member and my daughter—could no longer sit and listen to what she knew to be untrue. She abruptly left the room crying and returned only when she had regained composure.

When two hours passed and no resolution was in sight, the meeting ended. Without looking around the room, I picked up my folder, walked out the door, and headed straight for my car. Glancing back, I saw the women's team and all but one staff member following close behind. I didn't want to talk to anyone. Or feel their touch. Or have them say anything to me.

When I got into my car, I realized I felt no emotion. No anger. No pain. Even when one of the staff followed me to my car, reached into the car window, and sobbed on my shoulder, I felt nothing. No compassion. No grief.

One person later wrote that on that night she saw a "sacrificial lamb, yet a warrior strong and mighty, willing to submit to the battle of spiritual warfare." She added, "I looked over at Ann and a tear rolled down my cheek. I saw her as the lamb, and that broke my heart." But I didn't see myself as a warrior or as a lamb, only a woman called by God to lead and serve.

Despite the emotions that filled the room that night, I came to believe God wrapped me in a cocoon. His compassion and love protected me from greater pain, though I couldn't imagine the knife going deeper. He knew how much I could and could not absorb. He allowed the words to hit him rather than let them burrow into me. Did I hear the baseless accusations? Absolutely. But in the storm, God was my shelter.

Though the church leader responsible for the situation eventually submitted a formal retraction of the report, there was serious fallout. Yet through the uproar, God taught me some crucial leadership principles.

You're Not Alone

When the Spirit of God whispers, we need to listen. Though a decision may trigger a painful experience in our life journey, God assures us, "You are my servant, I have chosen you and not cast you off; fear not, for I am with you; be not dismayed, for I am your God; I will strengthen you, I will help you, I will uphold you with my righteous right hand" (Isaiah 41:9–10).

Two weeks before the report that sparked the explosive events, I wrote in my journal:

My life is yours, Lord. Teach me to walk in humility and love. Help me not to fear anyone or anything. Give me courage to go where you need me to go, to say what you need me to say, to write what you want written.

162

Little did I know when I wrote those words, what lay ahead and how it would affect so many people. But through it all, God reminded me he will never leave me alone because "he who promised is faithful" (Hebrews 10:23).

Your Obedience Is a Choice

When I desperately cried, "God, what do you want from me?" he simply said, *All I want is your obedience.* In that time, passage after passage of Scripture kept me focused. Verses like, "In returning and rest you shall be saved; in quietness and in trust shall be your strength" (Isaiah 30:15). I knew that no matter what happened, I was not to defend myself. I was simply to stand firm and trust the one who called me. But choosing to be still and quiet in the middle of accusations is not natural. And it's hard for others to understand why we don't "set them straight."

It's in crisis that we can be a light to those who look to us for leadership. Let them see that it is God who fights for us. Let them see that when we choose to be obedient, all glory goes to him. Satan is our enemy—not each other. He will try to destroy whatever God built up or accomplished in and through us. But "it is God who works in you, both to will and to work for his good pleasure" (Philippians 2:13).

We can choose to fight, or we can choose to pray a prayer similar to the one I wrote in my journal during those stretching months:

Father, you are wisdom and peace and love. Be those things through me, and forgive me when I fail. If anything in me could hinder your work, please reveal it to me. Give me patience and grace for those who may not agree with me and boldness to stand on what is truth. Fill me with your Spirit so others see you in me.

Your Focus Matters

How we lead affects others. Will we fight in a way that divides or destroys? Or will we, as servant leaders, shepherd others as he shepherds us, not leaving the door open for the wolf to come and devour the sheep?

During the six months of turmoil that followed that initial report with its resulting condemnations, I wanted to run. My heart ached and my mind raced, thinking that everything the team had put their hearts to meant absolutely nothing. I questioned if it had been worth it all. Yet, I knew better. The positive evidence was unmistakable in redeemed and changed lives. I also knew that if I left the church, others had told me they would follow. And I wouldn't be responsible for that.

Though no longer on staff, I continued attending church and tried to focus on encouraging the women who had served alongside me. Other people in our lives were also wrestling with what had transpired, and I believed the healing had to begin with us. But the team was hurting and deflated.

Following that September 2008 joint meeting, the team carried on with the previously scheduled weekend planning retreat, though it was unlike previous getaways. Pain and tears replaced the usual fun and anticipation we'd experienced in the past. Now it was time to focus on restoring our souls and renewing our minds.

When the road gets tough, it's easy to think we'll feel better if we simply put the pain behind us and get busy. But in our efforts to forge ahead, we risk avoiding what God wants to teach us in the middle of the storm. Or maybe we limp along or want to give up because it hurts too much. When we keep our eyes on Christ the Solid Rock, we can be confident that he filters everything before it comes to us. When we're experiencing what he has allowed, he's right there with us.

Focus on the one whose grace is sufficient (2 Corinthians 12:9).

Lean into his character—his love and faithfulness. See other people and circumstances through his eyes. And never give up. His grace is sufficient (2 Corinthians 12:9).

Your Hope Is Eternal

Over and over, God admonished his people to remember what God had done in their past so they would trust him with their future.

When we remember what God has done, he fills our minds with affirmations of his grace and love. Our thinking changes from defeat to victory and from impossibilities to possibilities. What he did in our past gives us hope for our future and strength to move on. Memories of God's faithfulness in our lives give us strength to carry on. He restores our souls and renews our minds so our steps find new life to move forward.

In the storms and struggles, know that you are not alone. Be obedient to him and know that he will direct your steps from beginning to end. Focus your heart and mind on God and know he will not let you go. Your hope is not in a title or in what you do. It's in the eternal hope that is found only in him.

At a Crossroad

God can. God does. And God will.
—Eileen Neufeld

In the heat of the devastating six-month storm that became one of the toughest experiences of my ministry life, many words of encouragement helped spur me on. Among them was a card from a friend and colleague who had a front-row seat to the goings-on. I share it here to encourage you:

> We don't understand why you are enduring so much right now, but we know you are not alone. You are in the palm of God Almighty. Imagine yourself there, close to his heart, and rest. May your heart heal with the strength of God.

In all honesty, the journey tested my commitment to the local church, caused me to question God's calling on my life, and affected the women's leadership team. Though I was no longer on staff or had a title, the church board still wanted me to continue working with the women of the church. At that point, I had a choice.

My head said, "Are you kidding? How can they expect that?" My heart said, "I need time to heal, and what about the others who are hurting?" But the real question I had to ask myself was whether I was here for the position or here out of obedience to God's call.

In the battle between my head and heart, I soon came to understand that God was saying, "This is where I want you to serve for now." And so, I continued to work with the incredible team of women God had called to serve with me years before. In the coming months, he never stopped showering us with his love and faithfulness as we lifted the church and each other before the Lord and sought his wisdom and discernment.

While we maintained some activity during those demoralizing six months that brought us to the end of 2008, what followed reminded me that, "A bruised reed he will not break, and a faintly burning wick he will not quench" (Isaiah 42:3). This was God's ministry and God's church. It was all for his glory. All he required of us was, "to do what is right, to love mercy, and to walk humbly with our God" (Micah 6:8 NLT).

Because of some moves to different cities or churches, the team saw a couple of changes. But as we recommitted ourselves to serve, we saw women grow in their walk with God and make a difference in the lives of their families and others. And we saw hurting hearts heal.

Leading into 2009, women continued to come alongside one another. As we considered how we could all be more intentional in our relationships, the idea to teach basic mentoring principles and skills took root. We didn't know how much interest there would be but, in addition to other Bible studies, we offered an eight-week study called Mentoring 101: Friendship with Purpose. Women could sign up for either a morning or evening class. If enough signed up to fill just one class, we would make it available. What happened next astounded us and launched another leg of our journey.

First, there were enough sign-ups to fill two classes—morning and evening. That was wonderful. Second, we had no book or guide on the subject and only one week to come up with something before the first class. That was a major challenge.

As the initial idea came from Donna Inglis and myself, we looked at each other, shrugged our shoulders and said, "Well, guess we'd better get to work." And work we did. For the eight weeks of the study, we brainstormed ideas, drafted outlines, wrote materials, and prayed—a lot. Each week, we wrote a lesson, made last-minute edits to handouts, and wished the printer would spit the materials out faster. It was always a race to complete everything before we rushed out the door to meet with the women who were waiting for the next lesson. Little did we know God was using this to redirect our path.

About the time we were nearing the end of the series, I was playing on a worship team at a singles conference where an author friend was teaching a workshop. When we sat down to catch up, during the only break we both shared, I told her about the mentoring study series Donna and I were working on. When I told her that people were suggesting it could be a book and I was wondering what to do with the material, she recommended a writers' conference that was coming up. Less than two months later, Donna and I loaded our luggage into the trunk of the car to head for the conference.

"Wait," Donna said. "We should take our binder of mentoring lessons with us—just in case."

"In case of what?" I shot back.

"I don't know. I just think we should take it."

Having been at a couple of writers' conferences years before, I knew we weren't anywhere near ready to present to an agent or editor. Our plan was simply to attend the conference to explore writing and Christian publishing. But I didn't argue. I ran into the house and grabbed the disheveled binder, then ran back to the car, and literally threw it in the trunk.

When we registered for the conference, we didn't sign up to meet with an agent or editor because times were limited, and I didn't think we were ready to meet with them. On the opening evening, we attended our first workshop, which was being led by a woman from a Christian publishing company. About a quarter of the way into her presentation, I had the overwhelming sense that I must talk with her.

We're just here to explore possibilities, I argued with myself. But the persistent nudging continued until I leaned over, whispered to Donna, and nodded toward the front of the room.

"I'm going out to sign up for a meeting with her. I'll be right back." Quietly, I slipped out of the room, claimed a time slot, and returned to the workshop. The next morning, Donna and I met with Athena and clumsily told her about our book idea.

Patiently, she listened and then asked, "Do you have your manuscript with you?"

After telling her we only had a binder with materials from lessons we'd been teaching for a Bible study, she asked, "Where is it?"

"Oh, it's in the car. But it's not ready for anyone to look at." I replied. "It's not a manuscript."

As I continued to resist, Athena turned to Donna and said, "She's a bit of a perfectionist, isn't she?"

We all laughed and finally agreed to meet again later that day—with the binder. As Athena sat across from us, she flipped through the pages, nodded her head a lot, and kept saying, "Aha. Aha."

As we sat politely waiting, I wondered what she was thinking.

After what seemed like a very long time, she looked up and smiled. "This really needs to be published," she said. "If you agree, I'll have a contract ready to sign before the end of the conference."

I sat speechless.

On May 2, 2009, we had a signed contract in hand and began our drive home in silence until I could no longer hold it in.

"Do you realize what just happened?" I said, as I turned to face Donna. "No one goes to a conference, presents a binder full of notes, and comes away with a signed publishing contract—especially an unpublished writer. It just doesn't happen. This is *all* God."

For the rest of the year, I continued with my coaching business and responsibilities to the women of our church; wrote almost every day to complete the book manuscript, and recognized that I was at a crossroads. God was laying out a different path for me.

In September 2009, I announced my intentions to step down from the helm of women's ministries in June 2010. The goal was to have a replacement by January 2010 and mentor her into the position. I thought a successor would come from within the team. Instead, the team dwindled.

Each woman had a legitimate reason, ranging from moving to a different city, to family or business issues, or pursuing other things God was leading them into. By February, it looked like only three of our team would remain after my departure. However, by March, God unexpectedly and quickly took Eileen Neufeld home to be with him. We were all in shock and felt the loss deeply. Now, there were only two of the eight members left to carry on. But by April, they, too, said they reluctantly had to step down. While most of the team committed to stay until the end of June, I couldn't help but look up and say, "God what are you doing?"

Sometimes, God has us involved in one area for a time and then says, *Okay, now you're ready to take this other path. I want you over here.* That was exactly what God was saying to me. Though the next bend in the road wasn't yet clear, I knew he was directing me down a different path. I was also learning to accept that even when a ministry ends, it can still honor God. Closure is okay.

God may not reveal his full blueprint, but when he lays a path before us, he asks that we trust him. When that path comes to a crossroads or fork, we must seek his wisdom to know which direction to take. No matter where the path leads, God will fulfill his purpose. His ways are perfect.

In March 2010, *A Mentor's Fingerprint: Leave a Mark. Make a Difference* came out. One year later, my second book, *Grandma's Fingerprint: Love a Child. Change a Life,* hit the bookstore shelves. Over the next few years, Donna and I launched Fingerprint Ministries and traveled many miles together—speaking at retreats and events and leading workshops.

In Isaiah 43:16–21, Isaiah challenged the people of Israel not to dwell on past miracles, such as the one they witnessed at the Red Sea. He urged them, instead, toward a new perspective and destiny. "Remember not the former things, nor consider the things of old. Behold, I am doing a new thing" (Isaiah 43:18–19). Through Isaiah, God wanted the people to change their focus toward the new things he was going to do. New miracles. Fresh paths.

God reclaims his own when we wander into a wasteland. He gives us courage in the storms. When he calls us to shift focus, it's all for his glory. He is our hope. For some of us, that change can be difficult. But when we're obedient, it's certain he has already cleared the way. In those new things, God gives strength in our weakness and equips us to fulfill whatever new thing he prepared for us.

"I will make a way in the wilderness and rivers in the desert . . . for I give water in the wilderness, rivers in the desert, to give drink to my chosen people, the people whom I formed for myself that they might declare my praise" (Isaiah 43:19–21).

Following my fifteen-year wilderness wanderings, God brought me back into church leadership. He gave me the privilege of serving alongside a women's leadership team of uniquely gifted women whom I grew to love and respect. Though some are now scattered to serve in other cities, churches, or ministry areas, our friendships endure to this day. Their willingness to be stretched and let God use the gifts and abilities he blessed them with was life changing. Their commitment to God and each other—on the mountaintops and in the deep valleys—was inspiring. Even in a mighty storm, they grew and stood as examples of women who deeply trusted God and reflected the character of Christ in their leadership. Together, God's love enfolded us. His faithfulness revived us. And his grace sustained us.

After four years of ministry with Donna, God brought me to a fork in the road where he made it clear he was about to show me a different path. And what a path it continues to be.

Since then, each bend in the road has been an adventure with him. My husband and I are still part of the body where God sheltered me through the greatest storm of my ministry life. He's allowed me to use the gift of music in church and beyond. He's filled me with words to encourage and challenge others while telling of his faithfulness through speaking and writing. And he paved the way for me to serve in a broader church staff role, helping others in ministry leadership. Life is full because God's faithfulness is real.

Over the years, I'm privileged and blessed to have worked closely with many amazing teams. Each step of the journey prepared me for the next, and each fork required a decision. Yet, God's love and grace were faithful and plentiful, always.

Though it's sometimes hard to let go, I'm learning to hold lightly to whatever God places in my hand because, one day, he may exchange it for something different. He knows the road ahead—every bend it will take, every fork it will present, and every bench it will reveal as a place to be still and rest for a while.

Wilderness. Sorrow. Joy. Loss. Victory. It's all part of the journey God created each of us to achieve for his purposes and to glorify him. Every part of our story is a stepping-stone to where God is taking us in his greater story. But God help us if we ever become so satisfied with how far we've come that we lose sight of how much farther we still have to go.

God expects us to do more than stand still at a crossroads or sit and warm a pew. When we stand still, we lose ground and slide backward while evil marches forward, trying to claim territory that belongs to God. We're encouraged by the apostle Paul's example to forget the past, look forward to what lies ahead, and "press on to reach the end of the race and receive the heavenly prize for which God, through Christ Jesus, is calling us" (Philippians 3:14 NLT).

Are you moving forward? Are you passing God's faithfulness on to future generations who will, one day, take up where you left off? Whatever God called you to, know that he placed you there to be an example of his grace and faithfulness. Walk humbly, knowing "that he who began a good work in you will bring it to completion at the day of Jesus Christ" (Philippians 1:6).

Long before our past became a memory, God carved out a plan for our present and our future. Our past is the past. As we release it into his hands, he redeems and restores it for his glory.

One Last Word

Our wounds and scars do not define us.

God blessed me with a godly grandma who nurtured and guided me toward the right direction. He appointed women and men to disciple me in my Christian walk and leadership. He also saw fit to let me choose poorly, so that I wandered into a moral and spiritual wilderness. There I questioned everything—my worth, my God, and the difference I made in the world. Yet through it all, he showered me with his amazing grace. He never let me go—not once. He was always there, ready to forgive and restore me to himself. On my journey back to him, I experienced victories and challenges, but he was forever faithful. Today I give him all the glory for the great things he has done and is doing.

The same can be true for you. God's hand was on you at the beginning of your life, and he sees you now. No matter where you are in your life journey, he is there. He never changes. He is faithful. You can, with God's help, emerge from the wilderness. You don't have to stay in that dark place.

But the choice is yours.

As you step toward the light of his grace, hold tight to our Father who holds you even tighter. In due time, you'll move forward more than backward. Your baby steps will cause you to lean into the one who never let you go in the past and will never let you go today or in your future. His grace is sufficient. His compassion is new every morning. You are still valuable to him. He still has a place for you.

> For this reason I bow my knees before the Father, from whom every family in heaven and on earth is named, that according to the riches of his glory he may grant you to be strengthened with power through his Spirit in your inner being, so that Christ may dwell in your hearts through faith—that you, being rooted and grounded in love, may have strength to comprehend with all the saints what is the breadth and length and height and depth, and to know the love of Christ that surpasses knowledge, that you may be filled with all the fullness of God.
>
> Now to him who is able to do far more abundantly than all that we ask or think, according to the power at work within us, to him be glory in the church and in Christ Jesus throughout all generations, forever and ever. Amen. (Ephesians 3:14–21)

With Gratitude

Each book written is a journey shared with others. It moves from the spark of an idea and rough thoughts scribbled in notebooks, to an outline and sentences that begin to resemble paragraphs and chapters. As edits and rewrites pass back and forth between author and publisher, the author struggles with doubts about the value of what they've written. But family, friends, and fellow writers urge them on until the manuscript graduates to layout and production—and a book is born.

I owe so much to so many for their encouragement, inspiration, and critique.

First, a special thank-you to the next generations of women who inspired me to write this book. It is for you, my daughter, granddaughters, and other young women, that I put pen to paper. When I was tempted to give up, the thought of you reminded me why this book had to be written.

Thank you to the different teams of women (and some men) I worked with through the years. The principles and lessons found in this book came out of the victories and challenges we faced together.

Thank you to my fellow writers in Writing Buddies for critiquing each chapter as it came off my computer. Thank you to the small team of prayer warriors who held me up as I wrote. And thank you to the awesome team at Redemption Press whose expertise and dedication helped bring the book to fruition.

Thank you to my friend and ministry partner, Donna Inglis, for your unconditional love, honesty, and wisdom as you endured the first draft of each chapter. And thank you to my husband and children for your willingness to be transparent as I wrote about a difficult period in our family's life. I love you so much.

Finally, I thank God for never giving up on me. He guided me with his wisdom to know what to say and what not to say. He nudged me with his Word when I struggled to find my words. And he gently pushed me forward with his unconditional love.

Notes

Other Books by Ann Griffiths

A Mentor's Fingerprint: Leave a Mark. Make a Difference.
Rich with real-life stories, guiding principles, and practical tools, this book will inspire, challenge, and encourage you to leave a lasting, positive mark on your circle of influence.

Grandma's Fingerprint: Love a Child. Change a Life.
This inspiring book is the poignant, gripping story of one woman's faith, courage, strength, and love in the midst of heartbreaking circumstances. It offers encouragement and hope and is a timeless example of the vital role that grandparents can play.

If you would like to share your story with Ann or invite her to speak at your retreat, conference, or event, visit her website at
www.anngriffiths.com

Endnotes

1. Ann Griffiths, *Grandma's Fingerprint: Love a Child. Change a Life.* (Enumclaw, Washington: Redemption Press, 2011), 191.

2. Bill Taylor, *From Infancy to Adolescence* (Belleville, Ontario: Guardian Books, 2007), 87–88.

3. Michelle DeRusha, *50 Women Every Christian Should Know: Learning from Heroines of the Faith* (Grand Rapids, Michigan: Baker Books, 2014), 252.

4. DeRusha, 239.

5. H.A. Walter, "I Would be True" (Public Domain, 1906).

6. Penny Gummerson, "Bottom Line," Business Monitor, October 1992, 7.

7. "The Strange Grave of John Milburn Davis, Hiawatha, Kansas," RoadsideAmerica.com, accessed October 14, 2021, https://www.roadsideamerica.com/story/2505.

8. Mother Teresa, quoted in Charles W. Colson, *Loving God* (Grand Rapids, Michigan: Zondervan Publishing House, 1983), 126.

9. Michelle DeRusha, *50 Women Every Christian Should Know: Learning from Heroines of the Faith* (Grand Rapids, Michigan: Baker Books, 2014), 65.

10. DeRusha, 105.

11. DeRusha, 266.

12. Thomas Ken. "Doxology" (Public Domain, 1674).

ORDER INFORMATION

CPSIA information can be obtained
at www.ICGtesting.com
Printed in the USA
BVHW070017011122
650615BV00004B/19